Jessi Mead

FINE TUNING
BARREL HORSES

Technical barrel horse training manual

**Jessi on her horse Chica, competing at the PRCA
rodeo in Steamboat Springs, Colorado.**

Dedication: This book is dedicated to all of the great horses that I have had the amazing pleasure of riding. Thank you for the tremendous sacrifices you made that allowed me to live out my dreams, and for teaching me how to appreciate life and push myself to be my very best. I will never forget any of you.

Jessi

Thank You:

To my daughters, Jackie and Raschel, for always being there to help with every aspect of the ranch and the horses. I could never have done it without you. I am so proud of the amazing women that you have both become.

To my mom, Fini, for pushing me to never be satisfied with doing anything half-way. **You are my hero**.

To my dear friend, Suzie Dow, for helping me with, and encouraging me to write this book; we did it. You are truly a great friend.

For information on Jessi Mead barrel clinics or her performance horse breeding program visit: **www.JessiMead.com**

CONTENTS:

INTRODUCTION
By Jessi Mead

As a competitor and a trainer, there is nothing more beautiful to watch than horse and rider working as one to complete the barrel pattern with total trust and flawless accuracy. And, in retrospect, nothing is harder to watch than a horse and rider struggling to understand each other and both walking away frustrated, confused, and angry.

I have been asked, time and time again, how I get my barrel horses competing at the top levels so fast and what kind of a training program I use. It took me over thirty years, two hundred plus horses, and a lot of experimenting with different ways of training to get where I am today as a barrel horse trainer. I have been able to refine my training program down to a unique set of training exercises and techniques that consistently work on barrel horses.

Because I am a visual learner, I found that when I was trying to learn a new training technique, in order for me to fully understand it, I needed to see all of the details of how it worked to completely understand why it worked. I also found as a trainer that I could significantly increase the horses' learning process by providing visual aids for myself. When I added visual aids to my exercises, it allowed me to give the horses more accurate and consistent signals, and give those signals at the exact same time, every time. By incorporating the visual aids in my training program, I was able to increase my horses' accuracy and consistency and decrease my training time.

So when I decided to write this book, I wanted to present detailed diagrams and training exercises that give as much visual aid as possible while providing plenty of written information, completely detailing the exact instructions to help the reader understand every little detail. Because I feel that understanding why you are doing something also helps you to understand how to do it correctly, I wanted to fully explain the exercises—the why and what for—to help the reader better understand how the exercises work.

While visual aids are extremely helpful to the rider, they are just as helpful to the horse. Horses are also visual learners, and they learn faster if you can incorporate visual aids in the training process for them. I found that it helped the horse to better understand what I wanted from him if he had a visual aid of some kind to make my instruction clearer.

When I added visual aids to my training exercises and techniques, I was able to teach my horses to be more consistent and accurate. I reduced the training time so significantly that over the years I have developed a unique set of training exercises and techniques that incorporate visual aids for the horse as well as the rider. By limiting my barrel horse training to these unique exercises and techniques, I have been able to produce consistent and successful barrel horses in half the time that it used to take me.

For this book, I have broken down the exercises to give detailed how-to information that is easily interpreted by even a novice rider. From the beginner to the accomplished professional, and the barrel prospect to the finished barrel horse, these training techniques and exercises will help both horse and rider improve their communication and riding skills so that they can make those flawless barrel runs with consistency.

Not everyone can afford to—or wants to—go out and buy an already fine-tuned barrel horse. They would, however, like to know how to make the horse that they already have perform at its very best. This book is a how-to training manual for all of these barrel racers. It allows them to improve the horses they already have, by giving them the training tools to fine-tune their own horses and get them performing at their absolute maximum ability.

While there are a lot of barrel racing books on the market today, I find they are mostly about the person writing the book and their accomplishments. They also focus on such a wide variety of barrel racing-related subjects—like the breeding of barrel horses, the conformation of barrel horses, basic horsemanship, and the equipment used for barrel horses—that there is very little technical information on how to actually train and fine-tune a barrel horse. There is virtually nothing on the actual barrel pattern in these books or on actual barrel racing concepts. These books are one hundred fifty to two hundred pages long but have only twenty to forty pages of actual information on how to train your horse or run the barrels correctly, resulting in incomplete information and vague details.

All of these books stress the importance of consistency, but they don't give you very much detail on the training techniques that teach the rider how to be consistent when training; they suggest only repetition for teaching the horse to be consistent. While repetition is a great tool for training, if the repetition is not consistent, it just confuses the horse. One of the most important parts of barrel racing is understanding the actual barrel pattern. None of these books give you actual barrel pocket measurements or teach you how to measure the barrel pockets to know where exactly to run your horse on the pattern to ensure the fastest run mathematically possible.

While I agree that the bloodlines play a large part in producing the correct conformation and athletic ability in barrel horses, even the finest-bred barrel Horse cannot perform at its best without the proper training.

What makes my book completely different from the other barrel racing books available today is that it breaks the barrel pattern down with mathematics, geometry, physics, and science to allow you to work on and completely understand each element of the barrel pattern, one part at a time. Then it shows you in detailed, easy to follow, step-by-step instructions how to take that information and use it to determine where and what you and your horse need to work on. It also shows you how to apply that information to correct the problems you have identified. And finally, it gives you and your horse visual aids to enhance the learning process while increasing the consistency of your run and the accuracy of your commands.

The training techniques in this book have come from thirty years of trial and error that have taught me what makes one training technique better than another. I have kept the ones that work the best and gotten rid of the ones that take too much time or are ineffective. These unique training techniques have allowed me to get everything out of my horses that they are physically capable of, and these techniques consistently helped me to produce champion after champion in the barrel racing industry, in a relatively short amount of time. These training techniques and exercises are the tools that have helped me to be so successful over the years.

If you see me out on the trail, please feel free to let me know what you think of this book. I am always open to new ideas and tools to put in my toolbox of knowledge. One never knows it all; there is always a new training technique to add to your toolbox of knowledge. I hope this book can help fill up yours.

Happy trails.

Jessi Mead

BARREL RACING CONCEPTS

The basic concept of barrel racing seems simple enough: run your horse around three large cans, be the fastest one to do it, and win lots of money. How hard can it be?

As the sport of barrel racing becomes more and more competitive, with just tenths of a second determining whether you get a check, the techniques used when running the barrels have become more important than ever.

Before we begin training on the barrel pattern we need to understand more than just the basic barrel racing concepts. We need to know how to streamline our training techniques in order to fine-tune our barrel horses to be competitive in today's arena. Also, we need to get rid of any misconceptions we may have, and understand the most common mistakes made in barrel racing so that we don't take any of them to the arena with us.

There are many ways to train barrel horses and most of them are effective, but not all of them are efficient. By breaking down the barrel pattern and looking at each part of it separately, we can determine exactly what needs to change to improve our time. Once we understand why we are losing time on the barrel pattern, the problem is much easier to correct. Also, by breaking the barrel pattern down into many different parts, you can see and better understand the mathematical elements involved in barrel racing, and learn how to use them to your advantage. Furthermore, working on specific problems, one at a time, allows us to make sure that each problem is corrected so that it doesn't cause additional problems later.

While all horses are not the same, they all have the ability to learn and improve, if their training is easy to understand and execute. The same goes for the rider; the rider can learn something new to improve his or her ability. The simpler the instructions are to understand, the faster the details can be learned accurately.

This book is designed to be easy to read and understand, and to be a useful reference tool when training. With lots of diagrams and easy-to-follow instructions, the user can flip to the section that covers a specific desired subject and find detailed help.

While there are many opinions about how to ride and train a barrel horse, not all of them are effective or backed with facts and experience. In this book, I explain why some of the "standard training methods" are not effective and how these misconceptions cause many of the common mistakes made in barrel racing today.

a.   Communicating with horses

In order to teach horses anything, we have to understand how to communicate with them. There are four commonly used communication methods that are available to us to help make our horses understand what we are asking of them. If we put all four of them together when asking our horses to do something, they are more likely to understand us.

First: horses learn from repetition, so we need to repeat our commands over and over to ensure that they understand exactly what we are asking them to do and exactly where we want them to do it.

Second: horses need clear and consistent signals when being asked to do something, in order to understand when the command starts and when it ends.

Third: horses are visual learners, so they learn faster with visual aids.

Fourth: and most importantly, we have to know how to gain the horse's trust. Your horse has to trust you before he can learn from you. By teaching through trust and understanding, and not fear, the horse is more willing to do whatever we ask of him.

When we put these four very basic training techniques together it makes it easier for the horse to understand what we want him to do.

Repetition: We all learn from repetition. If we do something over and over enough times, we will eventually get it right. The key to repetition in barrel racing is making sure that we do it the same way every time to get the consistency that we need. Repetition is one of the best training tools that we have, but if we are not careful to be exact when repeating a process, we can actually create confusion rather than understanding.

Consistency: The horse and rider both need to be consistent. Since the horse follows the rider's commands, the horse will be consistent if the rider's signals are given at the exact same time and place, every time. The rider needs to practice over and over to get the muscle memory necessary to be consistent in giving precise split-second commands and signals at the exact same time. The exercises in this book are designed to help the rider practice consistency without burning the horse out on the barrel pattern, while allowing the rider to teach the horse to be consistent without getting bored.

Visual: Since horses learn faster with visual aids, I have filled this book with visually aided exercises to help the rider increase the horse's ability to understand. These visual aids make it easy to find and understand the correct exercise and measurements for the desired area you wish to work on. These easy-to-read and understand exercises also help you and your horse communicate with each other so that you both fully understand the exercise. Making the exercises visual for both horse and rider enhances the learning process while increasing the accuracy and timing of the rider's commands, which leads to consistency in the arena.

Trust: In barrel racing, the horse needs to have complete trust in his rider's ability to give him the proper command at the correct time. The horse needs to wait for the rider to give him the command to turn the barrel at the last minute, without questioning or second-guessing the rider's timing. If the horse starts to feel insecure with the rider's ability to give the proper command at the proper time, he will start to anticipate how to avoid that fence or wall that he is running toward at full speed, and start his turn before the rider gives him the command to turn. When horses don't have complete trust in their riders, they have to start making their own decisions, causing them to be insecure, anxious, nervous, and upset when asked to go into the arena to compete. Establishing trust and consistency in your training is vital.

The training techniques in this book are set up to be done exactly the same way every time, for both horse and rider, making the muscle memory more and more consistent with every practice session. They also help build the very important trust and accuracy needed for barrel racing. When you practice perfectly every time, you and your horse learn much faster and become more consistent in the arena.

b.   Visual aids

There are several kinds of visual aids used in training barrel horses; some are for the rider and some are for the horse. Visual aids are a great training tool when used properly, but if they start becoming a crutch, they lose their effectiveness. The important thing to remember when using any type of visual aid is to make sure that it is doing its job without you or your horse becoming dependent upon it.

Some of the most popular visual aids used for barrel horse training are cones and tires. I don't like to use either of these, as they are visual aids that could cause your horse to trip or stumble. Furthermore, your horse does not really learn where to go; he just learns how to avoid them. When you remove the cones and tires, your horse no longer has to worry about stepping on them and he goes back to his old habits. He has not actually learned where to go, he has only learned to avoid the crutch: cones and tires.

As a visual aid for the rider, I like to use lime as a chalk line to mark the barrel pattern with a trail so that the rider can see exactly where to go. You can get a bag of lime at your local hardware store for just a few dollars, and it will not damage the arena soil. If the rider has a chalked lime line to follow around the barrel pattern, he or she can be more consistent in placement of the horse, since the rider can see exactly where to make the horse go. The rider can also easily tell when the horse is not where he should be. The chalked lime line works better than tires or cones because the horse can step on it without tripping. In fact, the horse quickly becomes used to the chalked lime line, and doesn't even notice it is there after a while. With the chalked lime line, any wrong movements are caught by the rider as soon as they start and can be corrected immediately.

This visual aid is for the rider, but it makes the learning process for the horse come faster, as it eliminates any confusion by the horse as to where you want him to go. The rider is able to position the horse in the exact same spot every time, and with repetition, this teaches the horse to be consistent. This also allows the rider to put the horse in the proper position to start his turn correctly so that he will be able to keep his balance when things speed up. By teaching the horse exactly where to go every time and by being consistent during your training, you will help him to learn faster.

The chalked lime line helps the rider to see if the horse is actually learning where he should be going by looking at the horse's tracks. If the horse's tracks are not on the chalked lime line, the rider can tell exactly where the horse is off, and correct only the area where he needs correction. One of the great advantages of the lime lines is that once your horse has learned where to go and the lines are no longer needed, the horse doesn't notice any difference, and he continues to work the turns and the pattern as he was taught, instead of just trying to avoid stepping on cones or tires.

Visual aids for the horse are very effective when they are designed to decrease the horse's options. By using visual aids to help your horse to see where you want him to go, you make the learning process easier for him to understand. When the barrel pattern is set up in the open arena, your horse has many options to choose from when deciding whether to turn the barrel. The numerous options available on a barrel pattern in the open arena make this a difficult environment for the horse to start learning how to turn a barrel. While the barrel is a visual aid that the horse can see, it helps to also frame it with additional visual aids so that the horse's easiest option is to turn the barrel and not to go by it.

Over the years, I developed a great exercise for teaching horses to make a proper barrel turn. It has visual aids to decrease the horse's options and to teach the horse how to turn a barrel before he ever sees the barrels set up in the barrel pattern. By teaching your horse how to turn a barrel before you ever show him the barrel pattern, your horse learns what is expected of him when he comes to a barrel in the open arena. He doesn't have to decide at the last minute what he should do or what his best option is because he already knows.

c. Balance, power, and speed

Balance gives your horse the ability to use all of his power, therefore increasing his speed. Balance is also how a horse manages to make fast runs, stops, and turns without falling down. His conformation requires him to have the use of his head to keep his balance, so it is very important to make sure that you do not interfere with your horse's head when he is trying to stop and turn. By taking your horse's head away from him, you take away his balance. You need to learn how to use your body weight and your legs instead of his head to help your horse make his turn.

When you shift your body weight back in your saddle, you help your horse shift his balance to his hind legs to compensate for the weight change, and when you lean forward, you cause your horse to change his balance to his front legs. When you sit in the middle of your horse's back, he can use all four legs like four-wheel drive, giving him more power and allowing him to push and pull at the same time to increase his speed. By knowing when, where, and how to adjust your body positions, you can use the horse's balance to your advantage.

Rating: Your horse needs you to sit/lean back in the saddle seat to help him rate and set his hind end underneath himself. He needs to be able to shift all of his weight to his hind end in order to collect correctly. If you are leaning too far forward, your horse can't shift his own balance to allow him to set down on his hind end and collect, causing him to have to turn on his front end. This causes gravity to throw you even further forward, resulting in a bouncy, hard-to-sit, sloppy, and slow turn.

Turning: Your horse needs you to stay set in the middle of his back and out of his way while he is turning the barrel, until he is <u>completely finished</u>. This allows him to make a smooth, accurate, flawless turn in four-wheel drive. If you sit up too soon, it will throw your horse's balance back to his front end and cause him to blow out of the turn, lose speed, and not have the ability to push/fire out of the turn with both hind feet.

Pushing and firing out of a turn: Your horse needs you to lean forward with your upper body to keep your body weight from causing drag and resistance, but not until he has completed his turn. This movement allows him to pull with his front end while still allowing him to use his hind end to push and fire out of the turn and stay in four-wheel drive. If you don't use your body weight to help him with his balance, your horse has to try to leave the barrel on his front end only, causing him to push out of his turn one-legged and out of balance. When he is unable to push/fire with both hind feet out of the barrel turn, he loses valuable time on his run.

<u>**Proper Balance = Power and Speed**</u>

d.   Riding posture for barrel racers

Riding posture is very important in barrel racing. The effect of gravity on your body when your horse turns a barrel is tremendous, so if you are not in the proper position you cause your horse to lose his balance and make sloppy turns. Think of your horse as a teeter-totter with you in the middle. When you move your weight one way or the other, you cause the teeter-totter to go up and down. If you stay perfectly in the center, the teeter-totter is in balance. Your horse handles your body weight in the same way. When you lean forward, he has to change his balance to his front end to offset your body movement; when you lean back, he has to change his weight to his back end. But if you can stay perfectly in the center of your horse, he doesn't have to worry about you throwing him out of balance, and he can turn the barrel in balance and in four-wheel drive—the fastest and most powerful way for your horse to run. Correct body posture needs to start at the arena gate, when you are getting ready to make your barrel run.

First, your hands need to be in the correct position on the reins. Your reins need to be collected up in each hand to the spot you want them to be at when you start your turn. That way, when you get to the check point all you have to do with your hands is check your horse, drop your outside rein, grab your horn, and push back on the horn to brace yourself for the rate. By starting with your hands in the correct position, you can concentrate on the proper check point and body positioning without having to worry about getting your hands to the right spot to start your turn. By only tilting your head and shoulders forward during your approach to the first barrel, and not your body, you won't need to change or adjust your hand positioning on your reins when you get to the barrel to start your turn.

Second, you need to know how to brace your body for the g-forces, caused by your horse's abrupt speed change when he rates for the barrel. The g-forces that result from your horse rating the barrel are very strong. If you are not in a vertically braced position when your horse rates the barrel, you will be thrown forward, causing your horse to have to use his front end to turn on in order to keep his balance. To brace yourself properly, you need to use your legs to push down and forward in the stirrups, and push on your horn to press your butt to the back of your saddle seat. When your horse drops his hind end to rate the barrel, your body's natural reaction is to compensate for the movement and lean forward. Bracing your body to handle the g-forces from your horse rating the barrel allows you to maintain your vertical body position. You need to make sure that you do **not** lean forward when trying to encourage your horse to speed up. By leaning forward with your whole body, you make it even harder to prepare to brace yourself in a vertical position in time for your horse to set and rate the barrel properly.

Third, It is also very important to stay centered on your horse in the vertical position throughout the entire turn. This allows your horse to bend his spine and lift his ribcage to round his body as much as possible to make a smooth rounded barrel turn, and not a roll back turn. In order for your horse to keep his balance during his turn, you have to sit very still in the center of his back. By staying centered on your horse's back, you do not receive the g-forces caused by the sudden turn. This allows the horse to make his turn without your body weight throwing him off balance. In barrel racing, we call this "the sweet spot." Because you are in the very center of the turn, much like being in the center of a merry-go-round, you do not feel the full effects of the g-forces. When you are in the sweet spot as your horse makes his barrel turn, it feels like the turn is in slow motion. If you are not in the sweet spot, the turn will feel like you are on the outside edge of a merry-go-round, and the g-forces will pull against your horse and throw him off balance.

Fourth, when leaving the turn, you have to be careful not to interfere with your horse's ability to properly push and fire out of the turn. The rider's body can cause a lot of wind resistance and drag if it is not in the proper position. Once the turn is completed and you feel your horse start to push/fire out of the turn, you need to lean forward just enough to allow your body to keep from causing drag and wind resistance, but still allow your horse to use his hind end power to push/fire out of his turn. By just leaning our head and shoulders forward to a vertical position with the ground and by keeping our butts in the saddle seat, we decrease the wind resistance and drag felt by the horse. This still allows the horse to maintain the ability to use his hind end to push/fire out of the turn.

Fifth, vertical body positioning during the straight part of your barrel run is also very important. We only need to tilt our shoulders and head (not our entire body) forward to help break the wind resistance and drag. If we are not in the center of our horse, he has to compensate for our body position to maintain his balance, and he will not be able to run in four-wheel drive. It is the human body's natural reaction to lean forward on the run home to try to encourage the horse, but leaning forward actually slows him down because he has to move his balance to his front end to compensate for the rider's body position, and doing so, he loses the ability to use his hind end power to push. The rider just needs to tuck his or her head and shoulders enough to help with the wind resistance and drag.

Riding Posture

I like to use a stick horse drawing to show the rider's body posture and the horse's body posture and how they relate at the different barrel points.

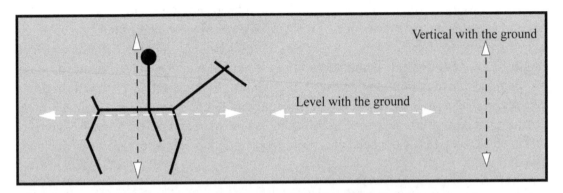

1-The running and turning body posture
Vertical body posture while your horse is running. The same vertical position is also used during your horse's barrel turn. This allows him to run and turn in four-wheel drive.

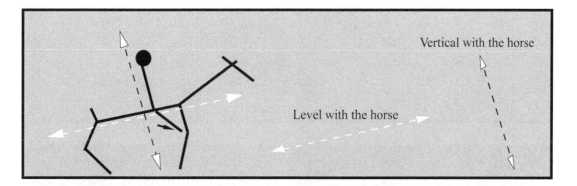

2-The rating body posture

The vertical body posture on a rating horse feels like you are leaning back, but you are not. The horse's hind end has just dropped to rate. You are still sitting level with the horse. You are able to brace yourself in this position with your legs by pushing forward and down in your stirrups and back on your horn.

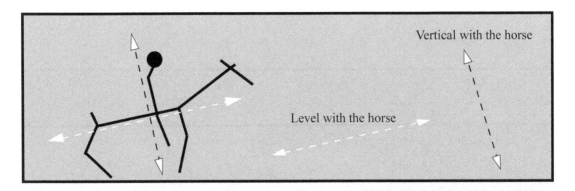

3-The push/fire body posture

This is the body posture of your horse when he starts to leave his turn and push/fire out of the turn. It actually helps your horse to lean forward with your shoulders and head to help him leave the barrel—but only use your head and shoulders. Do not lean your body forward past the point of being vertical with the horse. Keep your butt pressed down in the saddle seat; leaning too far forward or lifting your butt up out of the saddle causes your horse to lose his power to push/fire out of his turn with his hind end.

e.   Common misconceptions and mistakes

Looking at a spot on the fence when running to the first barrel: <u>Never do this.</u>
When your horse moves toward the barrel, the spot on the fence will no longer be in the correct place. You should be looking directly where you want your horse to go. Instead, while keeping the barrel in your line of sight, look about twenty to thirty feet ahead of you, through your horse's ears, to the spot on the ground where you want him to run. By doing this, you will help both you and your horse get to the barrel without taking extra steps. Your horse can't see where you are looking, but he can feel your body language; if you are looking off to a point in the distance, he will probably not rate the barrel properly.

Turning to look at the next barrel: <u>Never do this.</u> Always look only where you are going. Focus your eyes through your horse's ears, about twenty to thirty feet in front of you. Keep the next barrel in your line of sight, but only after you finish your turn. By turning and looking for the next barrel before you finish your turn, you actually shift your body weight enough to cause your horse to have to adjust his stride to keep his balance, and this adjustment usually takes your horse right into the barrel.

Kicking the air out of your horse: <u>Never do this.</u> By kicking as hard as you can, you only knock the wind out of your horse's lungs. Push your horse with your legs; don't kick him with them. Squeeze with your calves or spurs and stay seated. Never let your butt leave the saddle or your knees leave your horse's side. Always kick from your knees down. Large flapping kicks and letting your butt leave the saddle just throw your horse off-balance, and he will lose speed trying to compensate for it.

Whipping your horse at every stride on the way home: <u>Never do this.</u> This doesn't give him the chance to respond to the first hit, as it takes a horse at least one stride to make a change. You need to allow him to respond to every command before you repeat it. If you just keep hitting him, you are just giving him a beating. Failure to give him time to respond usually results in making your horse not want to come back into the arena. The best way to encourage your horse to finish hard is to use your legs to squeeze on him with your heels or spurs, all the way home. If you have spurs on, even bumper spurs, you can bet he will respond. If this is not enough and you still need to get your horse to finish his run, give him a slap on the shoulder a time or two. If a slap is not enough to get your horse going, you can use a quirt, a whip, or an over and under. You can use any one of these, but only once or twice on your run home. Be sure to wait for a stride or two between swats for him to understand and respond to your whipping him. You should not have to use a whip all of the time. I carry a quirt on my wrist for every run and rarely have to use it. But if I feel my horse cheating me on the run home, I have the ability to correct the problem right then and there. He will remember it the next time, and all I have to do then is lift my arm and threaten to get him to push all the way home.

Putting your weight in your stirrups too soon: <u>Never do this.</u> This signal lets your horse know that you are getting ready to go into the arena to make your barrel run. Your horse will start to get his adrenalin up to prepare for his run. Putting your weight in the stirrups too soon will cause him to wash out with nervous energy not knowing whether he is going to have to make his run now or later. By not putting your weight in your stirrups until you are ready to go into the arena, you help your horse to relax until the actual time for his run, and he won't be washed out.

Holding the reins too tightly pulled up when asking your horse to enter the arena: <u>Never do this.</u> This gives your horse mixed signals and causes him to get worried at the gate. Mixed signals with your reins at the gate will start gate problems. When you start to the gate, you need to be ready. Have your reins gathered up, but let your horse have his head with just minimal bit pressure. When you are ready for him to start his run, be sure to release all of the bit pressure.

Not sitting your butt in the back of the saddle: <u>Never do this.</u> If your weight is forward in the saddle when you ask your horse to rate a barrel, your horse will have to try to rate on his front end, which will throw you forward and even more out of position for the turn. Leaning forward in the saddle takes away both horse and rider's balance.

Sitting up and leaning forward before your turn is finished: <u>Never do this.</u> If your horse has not completely finished his turn, leaning forward too soon takes away his power to fire out of the turn and causes him to float out and bow off of the barrel.

Leaning and shifting your weight from one stirrup or the other: <u>Never do this.</u> This causes your horse to have to compensate and drop his opposite shoulder to handle your weight change. Shifting your weight to one stirrup throws your horse off-balance and out of position for a turn. It also puts undue pressure on the horse's withers and can cause your saddle to put his spine out of alignment.

Adjusting your saddle with your body weight: <u>Never do this.</u> If your saddle rolls to one side or another, don't try to roll it back by putting all of your weight in one stirrup and hopping on it. This can pull your horse's spine out of alignment and cause severe pain and damage to the horse.

THE BARREL PATTERN

The standard American Quarter Horse Association (AQHA) barrel pattern has a 45-foot shut down area from the gate to the timer line, a 60-foot start line from the timer to the center point between the first and second barrels, 90 feet between the first and second barrel, 105 feet from the second to the third barrel, and approximately 145 feet from the third barrel back to the timer line. The distance from the timer line through the pattern, around the barrels, and back to the timer line—with all of the angles—totals approximately 495 feet.

Some arenas have an alley for entering the arena, but the barrel pattern is always measured from the inside of the arena and not the end of the alley. Most arenas have center entry gates, but some still have side or offset entry gates.

Most of today's barrel races use an electronic eye to time the event. With only hundredths and thousandths of a second being the difference between first and second place, hand timing is just not accurate enough.

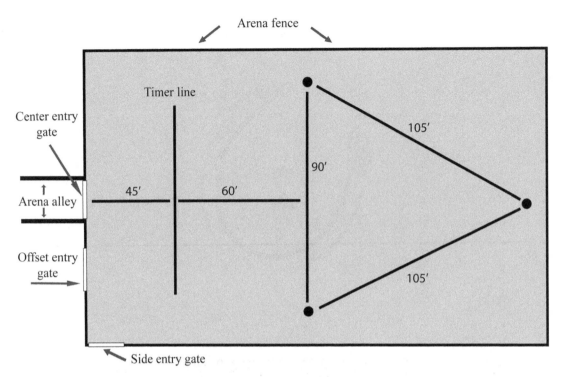

When you break down the actual measurements of the distance that the horse has to cover on a standard AQHA pattern—when it is run correctly—it totals approximately 495 feet. There is 65 feet from the timer line to the first barrel, 30 feet around the first barrel, 90 feet to the second barrel, 30 feet around the second barrel, 105 feet to the third barrel, 30 feet around the third barrel, and then another 145 feet back to the timer line.

To ensure a check at a barrel race in today's competition, on a standard AQHA barrel pattern, you need to complete this 495 feet in about 17.00 seconds. This makes every three feet that your horse runs worth about one-tenth of a second on a standard barrel pattern.

Not all arenas are large enough to set up a standard American Quarter Horse Association pattern. The smaller arenas have to make the pattern fit the size of the arena. This makes a fast time on these smaller patterns anywhere from 12 seconds on up depending on their size. The time loss per foot is even more than one-tenth of a second on the smaller patterns, leaving us an even smaller margin for error when we run on them.

In this book, we are going to take apart these 495 feet and determine exactly where we need to run in our cloverleaf pattern to complete it in 17 seconds.

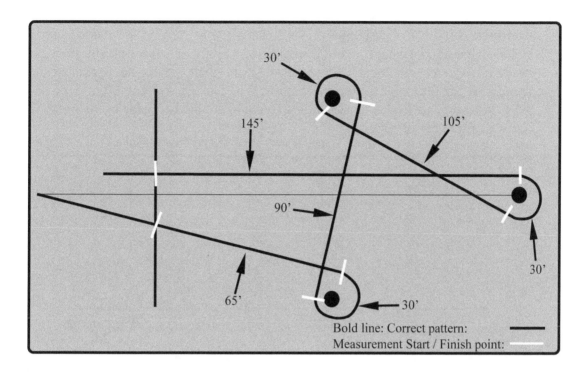

30'

145'

105'

90'

65'

30'

30'

Bold line: Correct pattern:
Measurement Start / Finish point:

a.   Shortest distance is a straight line

In barrel racing, every tenth of a second is important; you can be only a few tenths out of the fastest time and still not get a check. There is nothing more frustrating to a barrel racer than those last tenths of a second that just won't come off his or her barrel run. But if you know where to find those tenths and how to get rid of them, you will find yourself making more and more trips to the pay window. On a standard AQHA barrel pattern, every three feet you add to your run equals one-tenth of a second. Every time your horse doesn't fire out of his turn equals one-tenth of a second. Throwing your horse off balance equals tenths, improper warm-ups/washout equal tenths, lack of conditioning equals tenths, tired legs from hauling equal tenths. But the number one time clock enemy is incorrect pocket size around your barrels and not running straight lines to your barrels, between your barrels, and on the run home.

1) **Common first barrel mistake** = Taking too large a pocket and changing the entry point of the turn. This only adds time to your run and can cause your horse to start rolling back, stalling out, and hitting barrels.

2) **Common second barrel mistake** = Running straight to the barrel and then moving your horse over to start your barrel pocket. This not only adds time to your run, it encourages your horse to turn in front of the barrel and head for home. Another common second barrel problem is not staying seated until your horse finishes his turn, causing your horse to float out off the barrel, increasing the distance from the second barrel to third.

3) **Common third barrel mistake** = Not finishing your turn on the second barrel
    and blowing out, bowing the line from second to third. This causes you to come
    into third at an arc, and most horses will try to start their turn too soon, not rate the
    barrel, and run through the third barrel turn. When your horse doesn't rate, he has
    to try to turn on his front end and ends up bowing out the back side of the turn and
    coming off the barrel wide.

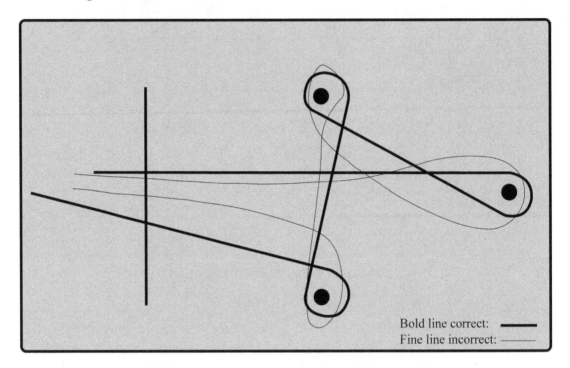

Bold line correct: ▬▬▬
Fine line incorrect: ───

b.   Barrel pattern entry point

The point that you enter the barrel pattern is also very important. If there is a center alley or gate, you will probably be set up to enter the pattern correctly. But when you know the best entry point to enter the pattern, the entry gate location won't matter. Imagine a straight line down the center of the arena; it should go directly to the third barrel. You never want to cross this line prior to going to your first barrel. When there is a side entry or offset entry gate, be sure to get your horse lined up on the centerline before you start your barrel run.

Since the shortest distance between two points is a straight line, you should always run directly to your pocket start point, no mater how far down the arena the barrels are set.

1)   If you try to move over too close to your first barrel, you will change the entry angle to the first barrel, and your horse will be out of position for the turn. This will cause him to stall out in order to make the turn, losing his continuous motion and valuable time.
2)   If you stay close to the centerline too long when running to the first barrel, you add distance and time to your run, and change your entry angle to the first barrel. This usually causes your horse to try to roll back on his turn, which often results in a hit barrel.
3)   If you start on the far side of the centerline, you are just adding unneeded distance and time to your run. This also changes the angle that your horse enters the barrel pocket, and he may try to do a rollback turn instead of a proper barrel turn.

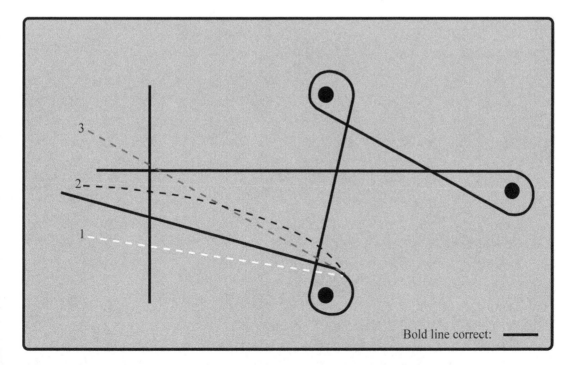

Bold line correct: ━━━

c.   Barrel pattern exit point

The point that you exit the pattern is also very important. With every three feet equal to one-tenth of a second on a standard pattern, you don't want to add any extra time to your run. Always remember that the shortest distance between two points is a straight line, and make sure that you are running straight until your horse has crossed the timer line.

1) A straight line from the point that you leave the third barrel is not always to the arena gate. Be sure to look at the arena before you start your run and determine where the point of leaving the third barrel in a straight line lands on the entry end of the arena. Make sure to run to this point and not just to the gate.

2) Once you cross the timer line, when you get to the end of your run, it is always best to circle your horse in the direction of his last barrel turn; this allows him to slow down gradually. This also keeps him from overreaching and hurting himself from trying to turn in the wrong lead.

3) Running your horse straight into the gate and then asking him for a sliding stop causes unneeded wear and tear on his hocks. We need to avoid stressing the hocks whenever possible to help keep our barrel horse sound, as the hocks are one of the first places barrel horses get injured or sore. Save your horse's hocks for the arenas that have closed gates and are too small to turn your horse in, when you have no other choice than to slide your horse to a stop.

4) Whenever you have a run out alley, always start pulling your horse up as soon as you are sure you have crossed the timer line. This may just save you from running into someone that might not be paying attention at the other end of the alley.

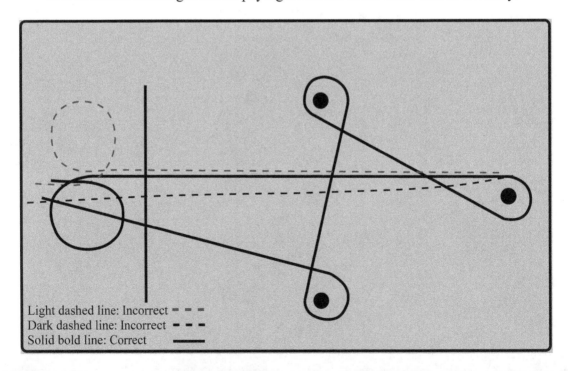

Light dashed line: Incorrect
Dark dashed line: Incorrect
Solid bold line: Correct

THE BARREL POCKETS

Before you can make consistent and flawless barrel turns, you have to know where your barrel pockets should start and finish. With every three feet equaling one-tenth of a second on a standard size pattern, the wrong placement adds precious time to your run. The pocket needs to be larger and further from the barrel at the beginning of the turn, since it's the fastest part of the turn. The end of your barrel pocket is the slowest part of the turn and more controlled, so it can be smaller and closer to the barrel.

By using the theory that the shortest distance between two points is a straight line, I have broken the barrel pattern down using science and mathematics to determine exactly where your horse needs to go to make the fastest possible run through the pattern.

Some horses need more pocket than others due to their size. Larger horses need a bigger pocket than smaller horses. Determining the correct pocket size for your horse is vital for allowing your horse the ability to turn in four-wheel drive and keep from stalling out during his turn. In determining the proper pocket start point for your horse, you have to take into account not only the horse's size but also which barrel you are talking about.

All three of the barrels have unique differences in the angle of approach, making the pockets for each barrel all look a little different from each other. If we draw a line showing the fastest possible run through the barrel pattern for our horse, we can see the actual pocket shapes and see the small but noticeable differences in the actual pocket shapes.

While first and second barrel pockets are very similar, there is a noticeable arc to the entry side of the first barrel pocket. The entry side of the first barrel pocket is slightly more rounded than the second barrel's entry point, which is straighter. This slight difference is because of the entry angle when we are approaching the first barrel. When you enter the pocket to the second barrel, you are entering it at a straighter angle than when you enter the first barrel.

The third barrel's pocket shape is very different from the first and second barrels, but the proper entry and exit points make the actual pocket around the barrels all the same size. And by keeping the turns all the same, no matter where the turns start or finish, your horse will become more consistent.

You can see the difference in the pocket shapes of the barrel pockets when you look at them in this diagram. While the first barrel pocket is only slightly different than the second barrel pocket, there is a very noticeable difference in the shape of the third barrel pocket.

While they all look different, from the actual start point of your turn around the barrel to the actual ending point of your turn around the barrel, The actual shape of the turn is exactly the same.

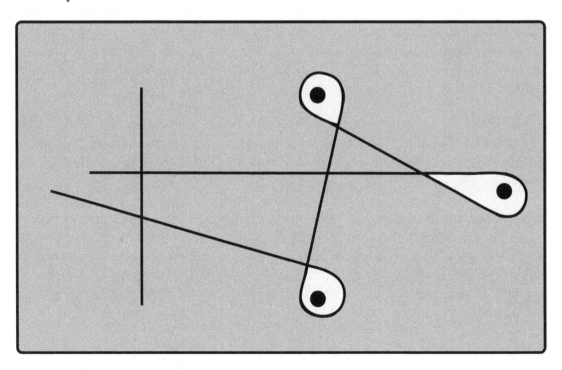

a. Measuring the barrel pockets

Every horse is a little bit different in size. Horses range from very large to very small; therefore, they all need to have a barrel pocket that fits them in order to make a proper barrel turn. By measuring your barrel pockets to fit your horse, ensures that your horse has enough room to turn the barrel properly without taking any extra steps and losing precious time. By marking your barrel pattern to fit your horse's size you provide a consistent and accurate visual aid to help ensure that your horse is not wasting valuable time in his turn.

You will need the following items to measure your barrel pockets.

1) **Your horse:** to determine the correct place to start your pocket.
2) **A stick:** to draw a line in the dirt. (A rake or shovel handle works great.)
3) **A tape measure:** that stays stiff/straight when laid out on the ground.
4) **Some lime:** to mark your pocket points. (A one-gallon coffee can works great to sprinkle out a line.)

This diagram shows your horse's placement on the barrel pattern for measuring the proper barrel pockets. The next few pages show you how to measure each barrel pocket in order to correctly mark the barrel patterns' pocket points.

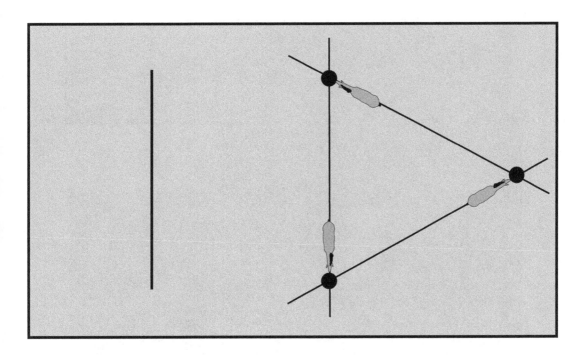

b. Measuring the first barrel pocket

To measure the proper pocket size for your horse on the first barrel, use a stick to draw two lines that cross in the center of the first barrel, with one of the lines going straight toward the second barrel.

Put your horse's nose to the outside edge of the first barrel with his butt pointed directly at the second barrel. The point where his tail drops to the ground is your pocket start point. This is point #1 for the first barrel.

Point #1 is the beginning of your pocket, or your pocket start point. (Point one is the total length of your horse.)

Point #2 is two-thirds the distance of point #1. (If your horse is nine feet long, then two-thirds is six feet. This is your point #2 measurement.)

Point #3 is one-third the distance of point #1. (If your horse is nine feet long, then one-third is three feet. This is your point #3 measurement.)

Point #4 is one-third the distance of point #1. (If your horse is nine feet long, then one-third is three feet. This is your point #4 measurement.)

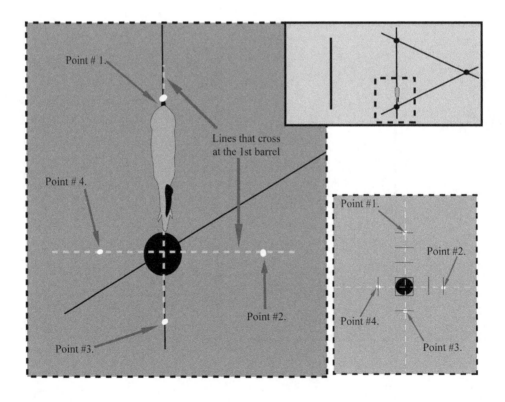

c. Measuring the second barrel pocket

To measure the proper pocket size for your horse on the second barrel, use a stick to draw two lines that cross in the center of the second barrel, with one line going in a straight line to the center of the third barrel.

Put your horse's nose at the outside edge of the second barrel with his butt pointed directly at the third barrel. The point where his tail drops to the ground is your pocket start point. This is point #1 for the second barrel.

Point #1 is the beginning of your pocket, or your pocket start point. (Point one is the total length of your horse.)

Point #2 is two-thirds the distance of point #1. (If your horse is nine feet long, then two-thirds is six feet. This is your point #2 measurement.)

Point #3 is one-third the distance of point #1. (If your horse is nine feet long, then one-third is three feet. This is your point #3 measurement.)

Point #4 is one-third the distance of point #1. (If your horse is nine feet long, then one-third is three feet. This is your point #4 measurement.)

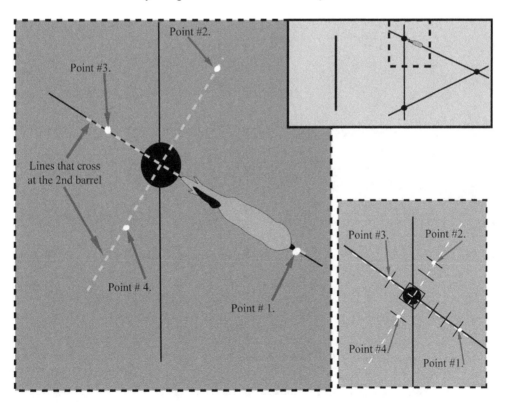

d.   Measuring the third barrel pocket

To measure the proper pocket size for your horse on the third barrel, use a stick to draw two lines that cross in the center of the third barrel, with one line going in a straight line to the center of the first barrel.

Put your horse's nose at the outside edge of the third barrel with his butt pointed directly at the first barrel. The point where his tail drops to the ground is your pocket start point. This is point #1 for the third barrel.

Point #1 is the beginning of your pocket, or your pocket start point. (Point one is the total length of your horse.)

Point #2 is two-thirds the distance of point #1. (If your horse is nine feet long, then two-thirds is six feet. This is your point #2 measurement.)

Point #3 is one-third the distance of point #1. (If your horse is nine feet long, then one-third is three feet. This is your point #3 measurement.)

Point #4 is one-third the distance of point #1. (If your horse is nine feet long, then one-third is three feet. This is your point #4 measurement.)

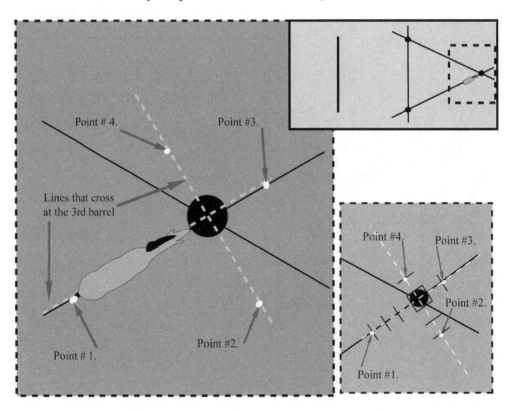

e.   Marking the barrel pocket points

Marking the barrel pattern helps you to be more accurate and consistent when you practice, by giving you a visual aid to follow while working on consistency. I like to use lime; it is easily found at most lumber or feed stores and is relatively inexpensive. Horses may look at it at first, but once they walk over it a time or two, they don't even seem to notice it is there anymore. This is the best part, because they don't use the lime markings as a crutch, the way they do with cones and tires. I use a gallon coffee can to shake out a little lime at a time to draw my lines.

1)   **First measure point #1** with your horse and mark the spot where his tail hits the ground. You can put your horse up once you have the first point marked with a spot of lime. Use a tape measure to determine the distance from the barrel to point #1. This is your point #1 distance. Now you can mark all of the #1 points with that measurement and your lime.

2)   **Second measure point #2;** take two-thirds of the distance from the barrel to point #1. This is your point #2 distance. Now you can mark all of the #2 points on the barrels using this distance, your tape measure, and some lime.

3)   **Third measure point #3;** take one-third of your point #1 measurement and mark all of your #3 points with a spot of lime.

4)   **Fourth measure point #4;** take one-third of your point #1 measurement and mark all of your #4 points with a spot of lime.

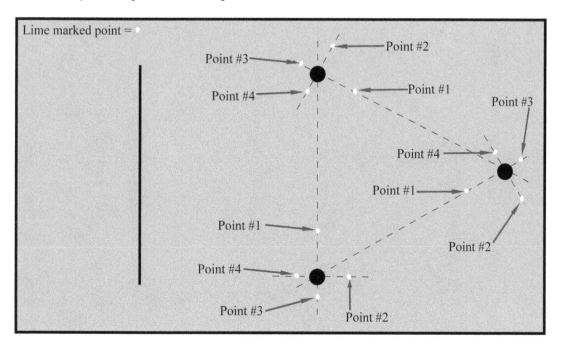

Connect the barrel pocket points. Once the points are marked, it is easy to connect them with your lime. Starting at point #1, and going in order to points #2, #3, and #4, draw an arc-shaped line with your lime to connect the points together and create a round shaped pocket.

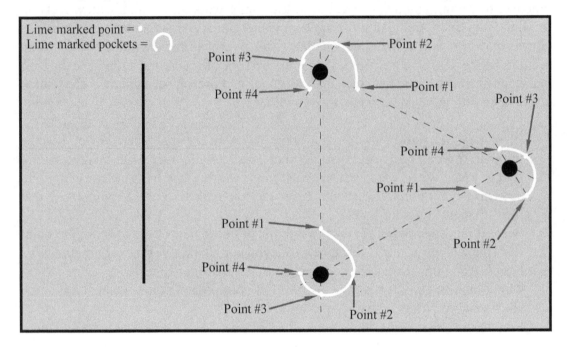

MARKING THE BARREL POCKETS IS THE SAME FOR BOTH RIGHT- AND LEFT-HANDED APPROACHES TO THE BARREL PATTERN

You just reverse the diagrams. All of the measurements stay the same. Marking the barrel pattern helps you to be more consistent when you practice, by giving you a visual aid to follow for working on accuracy and consistency.

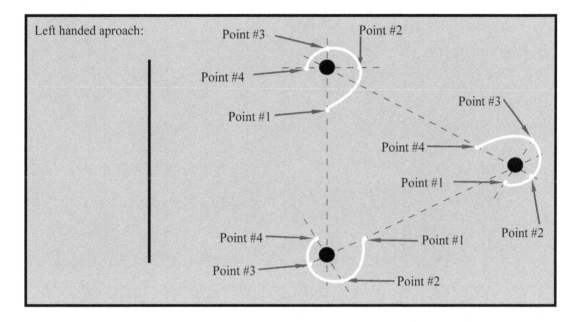

THE FOUR POINTS IN EACH BARREL POCKET

Check point, Rate Point, Turn Point, and Push/Fire Point

There are four basic points in every barrel turn: the check point, the rate point, the turn point, and the push/fire point. You have to know where these points are to help your horse make a proper barrel turn. And in order for your horse to rate and turn a barrel properly, you need to make sure to use your hands, legs, and weight correctly to help him and not get in his way.

Check: (rider only)

There are several different ways to check your horse. You can check your horse with your hands only, by pulling and releasing on the bit. Or you can check your horse by using only your body weight, leaning back in the saddle, pushing your legs forward, and putting your weight in your stirrups. You can also use your hands and legs at the same time, but it is important to always move your legs forward and put your weight in your stirrups to keep your balance and brace yourself for the g-forces caused by the horse's rate.

Rate: (horse only)

Once you feel your horse rate, drop your outside rein and push on the horn while keeping your weight in both stirrups. If you don't use even weight in the stirrups, you will cause your horse to be off balance, and he will have to compensate for it. This usually causes him to move one way or the other to keep his balance, and it changes your pocket shape, often resulting in a hit barrel.

Turn: (rider and horse)
Keep your inside hand forward and apply slight pressure by moving your hand away from your horse's neck to tighten your turn. Push your hand and rein toward the horse's neck to release the bit pressure to increase your turn radius. You can also use your inside leg if you need to increase your turn radius or move your horse over, but keep your weight evenly distributed by using your knees to hold on. Remember to always stay seated in the center of your horse. Do not lean forward until your horse has completed his turn.

Push/Fire out of the barrel: (rider and horse)
Remain seated throughout your entire turn; lean forward only after your turn is completed. It is very important not to lean forward too soon; this causes your horse to switch his power to his front end to keep his balance in order to handle your weight change, and he won't be able to push/fire out of the barrel with his hind end.

ALL FOUR POINTS ARE THE SAME FOR LEFT-SIDED APPROACHES
You just reverse the diagrams. All of the measurements stay the same.

a.   Checking

There are several ways to check (signal) your horse to rate. The most commonly used method is a quick pull and release on the reins. But it is very important that you also check your horse with your legs, by pushing your feet forward, shifting your weight to your stirrups, and sitting all the way back in your saddle's seat. The rider is also able to brace for the horse's rate by pushing on the horn with his or her outside hand, immediately after checking the horse. By giving your horse both check signals to rate, you make the command more understandable to your horse. And by bracing yourself while you are checking the horse, you will not be thrown out of balance when the horse does rates.

Check points for different horses

There are two basic types of barrel horses:
Chargy/run horses and natural rated/push horses.

There are four basic points in every barrel turn: #1, the check point; #2, the rate point; #3, the turn point; and #4, the push/fire point. Points #2, #3, and #4 never change, but point #1, the check point, changes for different types of horses. You have to know where these points are so you can check your horse at the correct point and so that he will be able to rate, turn, and push/fire at the correct points.

Chargy/Run horses need to be checked one extra stride before the rate point to collect to make a proper turn. Most chargy horses need only the extra stride on the first barrel, but some need the extra stride on the third. Most of them don't need the extra stride on the second barrel, as it is straight into a wall and they get a visual check on this barrel, causing them to start rating naturally, like a natural rated horse. The second barrel can be a problem for chargy horses because they try to slice it due to the visual check by the wall. Chargy horses will do much better on this barrel once they know their proper check, rate, and turn point.

Natural Rated/Push horses need one stride less than a chargy/run horse before the rate point. These horses use the barrel as a visual check point and check themselves. You have to learn to ride all the way up to the check point and still be able to stay braced and seated and be ready to start your turn without getting thrown forward when they rate. If you are not braced and ready when they rate, it will throw the horse off balance so that he can't make the turn properly.

b.   The check points

The check points can be in different places depending on your horse. Some horses need more time to collect themselves to rate a barrel; others run naturally collected and need less room to rate for the barrel.

The difference in the distance needed for chargy horses and natural rated horses is about one stride, approximately ten feet, between check points. But to determine exactly where the check point is for your horse, we have to determine how much space he needs from the time he is checked to the place he actually rates the barrel.

To determine where the correct check point is for your horse, you need to make one run to see where he is currently rating the barrel. Since the rate point never changes, we will adjust the check point until he rates at the correct rate point.

Take some lime and mark your rate point and starting check point. Then make a barrel run, check your horse at your marked starting check point at each barrel, and finish your run. Then go back and look at your tracks; look at your horse's skid marks (elevens) on the ground where he rated the barrel. If the skid marks (elevens) are on the marked rate point, then your starting check mark is good.

If your skid marks do not stop at your marked rate point, then move your check point mark accordingly. (For instance, if your skid marks are three feet in front of your rate point, move your check point up by three feet.)

If your skid marks do not make even elevens (both skid marks should be about the same lengths), then your horse is trying to turn while he is still trying to rate, and you are probably starting your turn before your turn point. Go back and make another run, and be sure to wait until you reach the turn point before you start your turn.

If your horse is still anticipating the turn and you are sure you are waiting to pick him up until the turn point, try moving your rate point back by one foot. Moving your rate point backward, away from the barrel, allows your horse to rate with both hind feet in balance before he starts his turn. When he rates his speed down correctly, he will be in position to lift his ribcage and make a proper barrel turn. Once your horse starts leaving even elevens on the ground he has figured out how to rate properly and is waiting to start his turn until he has finished rating. Now that your horse has learned to wait to start his turn until he has finished rating, you can move your rate point back up to the correct rate point.

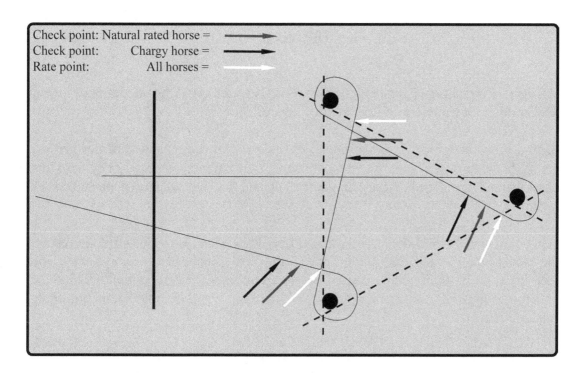

Check point: Natural rated horse =
Check point: Chargy horse =
Rate point: All horses =

**It takes a horse one full stride to respond to a command from the rider.
One stride at a run is equal to one of your horse's body lengths, about ten feet.**

**The check point for natural rated horses is approximately
one stride before the rate point.**

**The check point for chargy horses is approximately
two strides before the rate point.**

These are approximate measurements and meant to be a starting point. You should always take the time to determine where the correct check point is for your horse.

If you start having problems down the road with your horse going by the barrel, or anticipating the barrel and turning too soon, go back and recheck his check point. Once horses get going faster and gain more confidence, their check point may need to be moved. Just remember that the rate, turn, and push/fire points never change, only the check point.

c. The rate points

It is very important to understand the difference between checking your horse and your horse rating; they are two completely different things.

Rating is the action done by the horse; **checking** is the command the rider gives to get the horse to rate. This is where most people start having problems. They think that checking and rating the horse are the same thing and that they are both done at the same time.

When you check your horse to ask him to rate, he needs at least one stride to react to the check, or command, and rate his speed down. If you check your horse at the spot that you want him to rate and you do not give him time to react and get his hind end underneath himself to rate properly, he will be out of position to make his turn at the proper place.

Checking and trying to rate and turn at the same time will force the horse to have to start his turn before he has finished rating, which takes away his balance. This is what causes horses too start anticipating the barrel turn, and they will start going by the barrel or bowing out of the turn, losing precious time.

If you repeat this enough times, your horse you will lose his trust in you, and he will start anticipating the rate point himself instead of waiting for your command, throwing you forward and out of balance, since you may not be ready for him to rate yet. This also makes him anxious and nervous at the barrel, not knowing if he can trust you to give him the time he needs to ready himself for the turn.

These are just a few of the reasons that accuracy and consistency are needed at the check, rate, turn, and push/fire points.

The rate point is the spot where the horse sets his hind feet to slow his forward motion in order to make a controlled turn. The rate point is always at the same place. If you draw a line in front of the first and second barrels, a line in front of the second and third barrels, and a line on the back side of the first barrel and the third, you can see that your rate point is always where your tracks reach that line—and not just where your tracks cross each other.

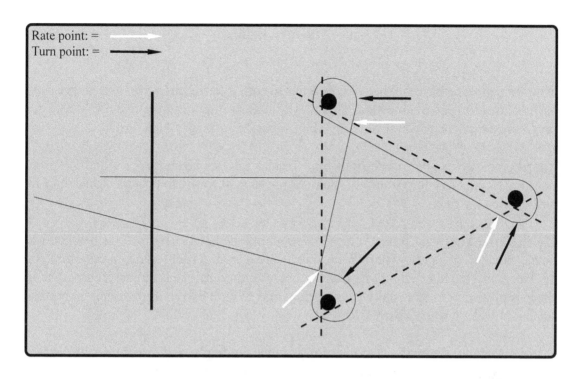

Rate point: =
Turn point: =

The rate point is one stride before the turn point.
<u>The rate and turn points never change.</u> They are always in the same
places for all horses, chargy or natural rated.
The check point is the only point that changes.
The rate point is one stride before the turn point.

d.   The turn points

Your horse has to have his balance in order to turn a barrel properly, and he needs to use his head to keep his balance. This is why it is so important that we don't take our horse's head/balance away from him when we ask him to make his turn.

Your horse also needs to use both hind feet to rate a barrel properly and keep his balance, so it is very important for the rider not to start trying to turn the horse until he has finished his rate.

If you start asking your horse to turn too soon, and he has to give you his head before he has finished rating, he will only be able to use one hind foot to rate, in order to keep his balance. This also usually causes the horse to do a rollback turn, which results in the loss of your pocket, usually causing the horse to hit a barrel, drop his shoulder, lose time, and make a sloppy barrel turn.

When asking your horse to start his turn, you need to apply light pressure to the inside rein, allowing your horse to follow his nose around the barrel. You should not have to jerk his head away to get him to turn. Doing so will only throw him out of balance, and he will definitely not be able to turn the barrel correctly.

The turn point is one stride after the rate point, and never until the horse has finished rating. Some horses' mouths are lighter to the touch than others. For that reason, the amount of pressure applied to the inside rein when asking the horse to start the turn may be different, but the turn point never changes. **Never start the turn before the turn point**. If you do not give your horse time to rate properly, he will not be able to lift his ribcage and make his turn in balance.

Body posture is also a very important part of your turn. You need to stay seated throughout your turn, never leaning forward until you have completed the turn. You also need to stay in the center of the horse; do not lean from side to side putting more of your weight in one or the other stirrups. During a barrel turn, your horse has to bend his ribcage. If you are moving around up there, he has to try to adjust for your movements and can't bend properly to complete his turn.

The push/fire point is after, and **only after,** the turn is completed and you have a straight line of sight to the next barrel.

The turn point is one stride after the rate point, and the turn does not finish until you reach the push/fire point.

It is very important to remember to release any inside rein pressure from your turn before you ever ask your horse to push/fire out of the turn. If you do not release the inside rein pressure and give your horse his head back, your horse will not be able to stretch out his neck to get the balance needed to push/fire out of the barrel properly, with both hind feet. When your horse can't push/fire out of the turn with both hind feet, you lose valuable time off the barrel.

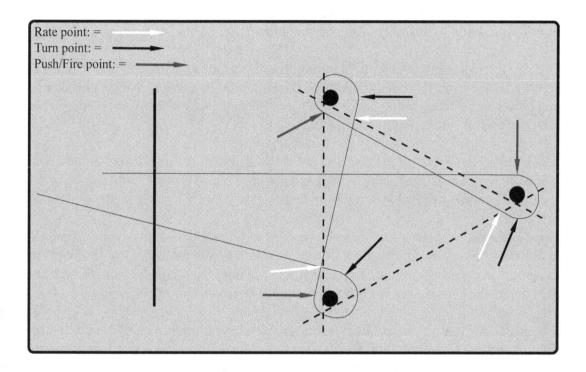

The turn point never changes.
The turn point is one stride after the rate point.
The push/fire point is only after the turn is completed.

e.   The push/fire points

The push/fire point is only after your horse has completed his turn and you have a straight line of sight to the next barrel.

We can help our horse to push/fire out of his turn with our body by leaning forward with our head and shoulders, but if we lean forward too soon or too much, we hinder our horse's ability to push/fire with both hind feet.

Our horse needs to push/fire with both hind feet to maximize his power and regain full speed after the turn. If we lean forward too much, the horse has to switch his balance and power to his front end to handle our weight change, taking away the power in his hind end to push/fire out of his turn.

When the horse moves his balance and power to his front end, he gains more power to pull with, but he also loses some of the power to push out of his turn with, and a horse's hind end is more powerful than his front end.

Once our horse starts to leave the turn, we need to tilt our head and shoulders forward to keep our body from causing drag or wind resistance from the horse's push/fire off of the turn. But we need to be sure not to lean forward with our whole body, as this causes the horse to lose the power to push with both of his hind feet.

We also don't want to just sit there and cause the horse to lose his ability to pull with the full power of his front end. By staying seated throughout the entire turn and only tilting our head and shoulders forward once the turn is completed and our horse starts to push/fire out of the turn, we allow our horse to use both his hind end and front end to give us his maximum power and speed.

It is also very important to never push/fire out of your turn too soon. If your horse is still trying to finish his turn when you ask him to start to push/fire out of it, you will cause your horse to have to blow out of the back side of the turn. And if you ask your horse to push/fire out of his turn too late, you will lose valuable time.

These are just a few reasons why it is so important to know when, where, and how to push/fire out of your turn properly.

The push/fire point is the spot where the horse plants both hind feet and pushes and pulls with all of his power to actually leave the turn and head for the next barrel. The push fire point starts only after your horse has completed his turn and you have a straight line of sight to the next barrel.

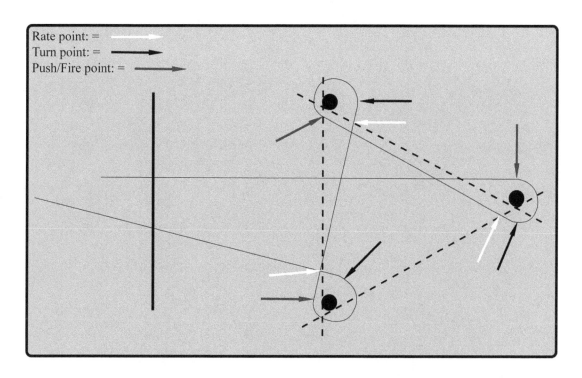

Rate point: =
Turn point: =
Push/Fire point: =

The push/fire point is only after the turn is fully completed.
Tilt only your head and shoulders forward to help
your horse at the push/fire point.

MARKING THE BARREL PATTERN
FOR TRAINING

Over the years, I learned that the more accurate I was in giving my horses their training commands, the more consistent they were on the barrel pattern. But it was hard to tell if I was being exact in the timing when giving these commands to the horse. I came up with the idea of marking the barrel pattern so that I could see exactly where to give the commands every time, and to see if it helped me be more accurate and consistent in giving the commands.

The difference was night and day. Not only were my horses more consistent when I finally started running them on the barrel pattern, they were also learning at an incredibly fast pace. What used to take me months to teach was now taking me only weeks, and it was not just a fluke. They really had learned what I wanted them to learn, and they did it exactly the way I had taught them, every time.

In this chapter, I go through the entire process of marking the barrel pattern for training barrel horses. And I have broken down the process of marking the barrel pattern into four sections so that each part of the process makes cense to the reader. I have found that if I have all of the little details, it is easier for me to get the whole picture and understand the overall process better. So it may seem like I am over explaining the process for some people, but I want to make sure that everyone understands the entire process and that I am not leaving any questions unanswered.

1) Marking the pocket points

2) Connecting the pockets, entry, and exit points to each other

3) Marking the four barrel points

4) Finding and marking the correct check points

5) The marked barrel pattern

a.   Marking the pocket points

In order to start marking the barrel pockets for training, you first have to measure the barrel pockets (this process is shown in more detail in Chapter 3 under "Measuring the barrel pockets") and mark the pocket points. Then you are ready to follow the steps below to connect the pocket points to form your barrel pocket.

First, measure point #1 with your horse and mark the spot where his tail hits the ground. You can put your horse up once you have the first point marked with a spot of lime. Use a tape measure to determine the distance from the barrel to point #1. This is your point #1 distance. Now you can mark all of the #1 points with that measurement and your lime.

Second, take two-thirds of the distance from the barrel to point #1. This is your point #2 distance. Now you can mark all of the #2 points on the barrels using this distance, your tape measure, and lime.

Third, take one-third of your point #1 measurement and mark all of your #3 and #4 points with a spot of lime.

Once your points are marked, it is easy to connect them with your lime to form your barrel pockets. Just make a line with your lime. Start at point #1 and go to points #2, #3, and #4 in order, to form an arc-shaped line connecting your lime marked points to each other and rounding out the barrel pocket.

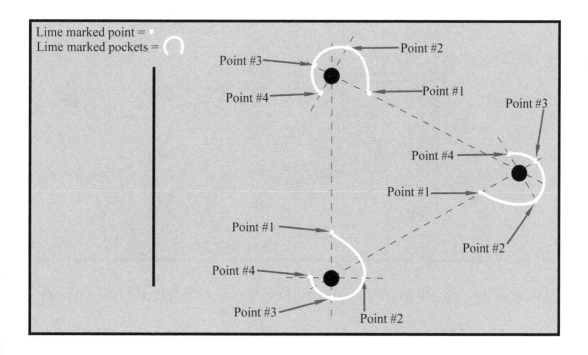

b. Connecting the pockets' entry and exit points to each other

Marking the pocket points first and using the marked points to complete your barrel pockets allows you to make the lines between the barrels as straight as possible to ensure that you are not wasting any extra steps.

Once you have measured and marked your barrel pockets, it is easy to connect the pockets to each other with a line of lime.

First, you start from your arena entry point and draw a straight line with your lime to point #1 of the first barrel pocket.

Second, you mark a straight line with your lime from point #4 of the first barrel pocket to point #1 of the second barrel pocket.

Third, mark a lime line from point #4 of the second barrel pocket to point #1 of the third barrel pocket.

Fourth, mark a lime line from point # 4 of the third barrel pocket to where your exit point crosses the timer line.

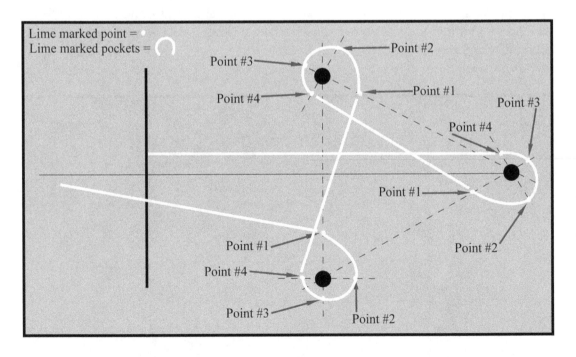

The lime lines connecting the barrel pockets to each other should look like this.

c. Marking the four barrel points

Now that you have your pockets measured, marked, and connected to each other, it is time to mark your barrel points.

a) Draw a line in the dirt with a stick that crosses the outside front of the first barrel, going straight to the outside front of the second barrel.
b) Draw a line in the dirt with a stick that cross the inside side of the second barrel, going straight to the inside front of the third barrel.
c) Draw a line in the dirt with a stick that crosses from the outside of the first barrel, going straight to the outside of the third barrel.

The four barrel points include the check point, the rate point, the turn point, and the push/fire point.

1) **Rate point:** Now you can take some lime and mark your rate point. Make about a ten-foot line with your lime that crosses the lime line that connects your barrel pockets to each other and the point where you drew the line with a stick.
2) **Check point:** Then mark your check point one full body length (from the tip of your horse's nose to where his tail drops to the ground) **in front** of your rate point at each barrel.
3) **Turn point:** Then mark your turn point one full body length (from the tip of your horse's nose to where his tail drops to the ground) **past** the marked rate point at each barrel.
4) **Push/Fire point:** Then mark your push/fire point. It is where your marked lime line starts going straight to the next barrel.

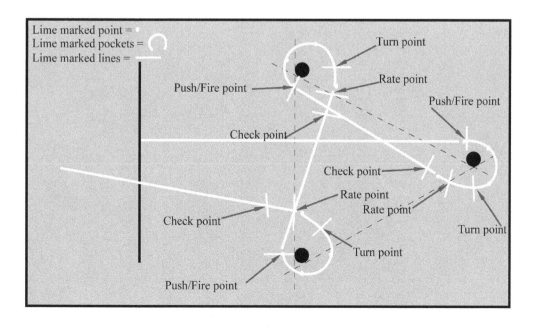

d.   Finding and marking the correct check points

Now that you have all of the points marked, you need to check to ensure that you have the correct check point marked for your horse. Once you have marked your barrel pattern, you can make a run to determine the correct check point for your horse.

You need to start out using one of your horse's body lengths as a starting check point to find your horse's correct check point. When your horse's nose reaches the marked check point at each barrel, check your horse and finish your run.

After you have made your run, go back and look at your tracks. Your horse will have left rate/skid marks (elevens) on the ground where he rated the barrels. If the rate/skid marks (elevens) stop on the marked rate point, then your check point marks are good.

If your skid/rate marks (elevens) are not on the correct rate point, then you need to adjust your check point to fit your horse.

To adjust your check point if the rate/skid marks (elevens) are past the marked rate point, you need to move your check point back away from the marked rate point, increasing the distance between the two points. Measure the distance that the skid marks cross over the marked rate point, and move your check point mark back by this measurement.

To adjust your check point if the rate/skid marks (elevens) are in front of the marked rate point, you need to move your check point mark toward the rate point mark, decreasing the distance between the two points. Measure the distance that the rate/skid marks are short of the marked rate point, and move your check point forward by this measurement.

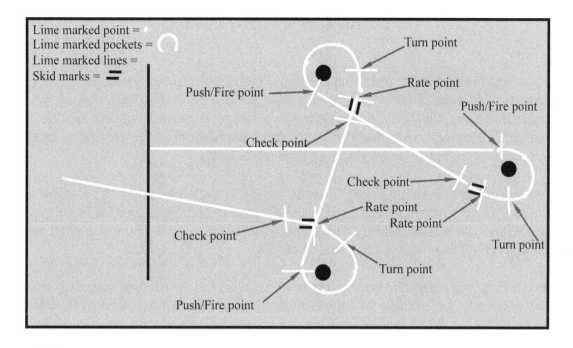

Lime marked point =
Lime marked pockets =
Lime marked lines =
Skid marks =

Turn point
Rate point
Push/Fire point
Push/Fire point
Check point
Check point
Rate point
Rate point
Check point
Turn point
Turn point
Push/Fire point

Finding the correct check point for green or young horses that are not running the barrel pattern fast enough to leave clear skid marks (elevens) is hard to do.

Therefore, for young horses that have not learned how to rate or are not rating hard enough yet to leave good skid marks, you have to use one full body length to determine your starting check point measurement. For most horses, I have found that this is the correct measurement, even after they get their speed up.

Once your horse is rating hard enough to leave good skid marks (elevens), you can use your rate point to check and see if you need to adjust your check point. If you need to move your check point, it is usually just a mater of moving it up by one foot or back by one foot; just be sure to remember to measure this new distance and change your check point mark on your practice barrel pattern accordingly.

e.   The marked barrel pattern

Once you have marked your pocket points, barrel points, and found your horse's correct check point, the marked barrel pattern is ready for you to start training your horse. However, you should never start showing a horse the barrel pattern, marked or not, until he knows how to work collected at a controlled speed, to work off your leg commands, and how to do a flying lead change.

Weather you are starting a young horse or fine-tuning an already started barrel horse, before you make a training run on the marked barrel pattern, you should halve already taught him how to make a proper barrel turn by working him on the proper barrel turn exercise. (Explained in full detail in Chapter 8.)

By teaching your horse how to make a proper barrel turn first, he will have already learned how to collect, rate, and make the turn around the barrel properly, so when you show him the barrel pattern, all he has to do is learn the actual location of the barrels in the pattern.

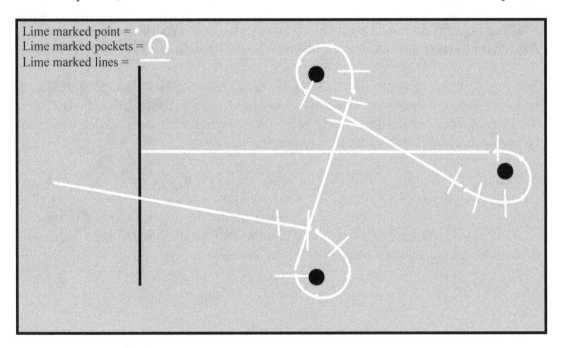

The marked barrel pattern should look like this when it is completely marked for training.

Correct horse, hand and body positioning at the check point.

Correct hand and leg position at the rate point.

Correct horse, hand and body positioning at the turn point.

Correct horse, hand and body position at the push/fire point.

TRAINING HORSES/PROSPECTS
FOR BARREL RACING

It is very important that your horse is broke for barrel training. Yes, there is a difference in broke and broke for the barrels. You don't have to hire a professional trainer to do this; you can do it easily yourself, but you should never start a horse on barrels until he understands these three basic training commands.

For a horse to completely understand that we are repeating the same thing over and over to teach him something, he has to do it the same way at least three times, just to recognize where the process starts and ends. So when I want to teach a horse a new exercise or command, I repeat it five times to ensure that he knows where the exercise or command starts and where it ends, and that he knows how to do everything correctly.

1) **Collection and controlled speed:** Horses that are going into barrel training need to know how to collect at the poll. In order to work and keep continuous motion while in a collected gait, they also have to work on a loose rein and give at the poll at all speeds. They need to be able to lope a circle in a controlled lope without the rider having to rate them down all the time with the reins, or urge them on to keep their continuous motion. They also need to be able to stay in their tracks around a forty to fifty-foot circle without changing speed. This is very important so your

horse can keep his balance and continue his forward motion throughout his barrel turn in control, so he doesn't stall out.

2) **Leg commands:** Your horse also needs to be comfortable with leg commands. If your horse knows how to work off of your legs, you can easily move him as needed and position him in the correct spot to start your turn around the barrel. You can also use your leg commands to make sure that your horse is in the proper place to enter his pocket without taking away his balance by pulling on his head. Using your legs to help position your horse will also keep you from getting your hand out of position for your turn.

3) **Flying lead changes:** Your horse needs to know how to change his leads while keeping his forward motion. Your horse may not be in the correct lead when he enters the arena gate and heads for the first barrel, so he will have to know how to change his leads on the fly, and most horses need to learn how to do a flying lead change. If your horse is in the wrong lead before he starts to turn a barrel, he will have to try to turn the barrel in the wrong lead, causing him to blow out of the back side of the turn. Trying to turn in the wrong lead also usually causes your horse to overreach and injure himself.

a. Collection and controlled speed

Teaching your horse how to collect is one of the most important parts of barrel horse training. Collection is different than rate. When a horse rates, he gathers his hind end and plants his hind feet to slow down his forward motion. When a horse collects, he breaks at the poll, allowing him to get his legs in control underneath him and continues his forward motion.

A horse that is working collected continues his forward motion without planting his hind legs to reduce his speed. When a horse is in a full-out run, he is stretched out and his ability to make quick turns is limited, but he is able to run at his top speed. When he is running in a collected gait, he has much better control of his legs for quick sudden movement like barrel turns, but he is not able to reach his top end speed while collected.

In order for a horse to gather his legs from a full-out run and continue to run at a collected speed, he has to give at the poll and gather his legs underneath himself to keep his balance. Once a horse has learned how to collect from a full-out run, he is able to rate and turn a barrel in balance with extreme accuracy.

Some horses naturally know how to gather and collect themselves to rate the barrel, but most of them need to learn. In order for your horse to learn how to collect himself up and rate his speed down, he needs to be comfortable with collecting himself up from a full-out run without stopping. Teaching your horse how to control his speed while keeping his continuous motion is very important in barrel racing because we only want him to slow down enough to keep his balance while he makes his turn.

Horses have to be shown everything on each side and in each direction separately. Like when you get on your horse, if you get up on him from only one side, you have to teach him that it is OK to let you get up on the other side. The same thing works when teaching him to do a right or left-hand turn. You may think that because you have taught him to make a correct barrel turn to the right, that he knows how to do the same to the left. This is not the case; you have to show him how to do both turns separately.

When we work our horses on the barrel pattern, they get only one right-hand turn, but they get two left-hand turns. Therefore, the one right-hand turn gets practiced only half as much as the left-hand turn. This is also the same for the rider's commands, we only give the right hand turn commands once and the left-hand turn commands twice, making our muscle memory to the left more consistent than our muscle memory to the right.

We all have a dominant side, leg, or hand, and we may not be giving the exact same command when we ask our horse to turn to the right as we do when we ask him to turn to the left. So we have to practice and train our bodies so that they have the same muscle memory on both sides.

b.   Teaching collection and controlled speed
(continuous motion circles)

This exercise helps us to build consistent muscle memory on both sides when practicing our turns. It allows the rider to work each side of his or her body evenly by giving the same commands to the horse over and over, several times in the same direction, and then change directions and give the same amount of commands to the other side to help develop muscle memory equally.

This exercise also works both of the rider's hands and legs evenly with the same amount of time in each direction, and helps both the horse and the rider develop evenly and create balanced muscle memory for greater consistency. And if the horse has a dominant side, the rider can use this exercise to focus on his weak side.

This exercise may seem too simple to be of much value, but its simplicity helps you teach your horse how to work collected at the poll in a controlled gait while the rider works on his or her muscle memory and hand and body positioning. This exercise also allows the horse and rider to have to think only about a few things at a time so that they can focus on getting it all correct without stressing out. This exercise can be done at all speeds to allow your horse to get comfortable with working in a collected lope or run, and it is simple enough that it can be done over and over to give both the horse and rider a chance to learn from repetition without burning out.

This exercise also teaches your horse to stay in the correct lead and keep his continuous forward motion while using his hind end power to push and his front-end power to pull. Once the horse learns how to lope and run in four-wheel drive, he also learns how to turn without dropping his inside shoulder.

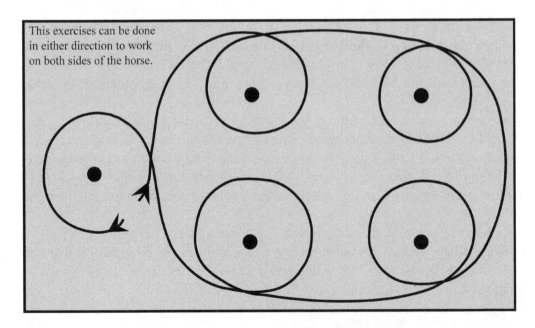

This exercises can be done in either direction to work on both sides of the horse.

c. Teaching push/fire
(the corkscrew)

This exercise helps teach your horse to relax and concentrate on turning in four-wheel drive before asking him to leave his turn and push/fire away from the barrel. It also helps keep your horse gathered, collected, and in the correct position for a barrel turn. Your horse has to learn how to turn in four-wheel drive and keep forward motion while turning without stalling out to make a proper barrel turn and not an oval rollback turn.

This exercise should be done at a lope and not a full-out run. It is designed to be used to teach control, not speed. Your horse needs to start out in a large circle and learn to collect before he can turn a small circle collected. Your horse also needs to learn how to leave the turn with a powerful push/fire out and away from the barrel. This exercise works great to teach the horse to push/fire out of the turn when he is in a collected turn. It also helps you to feel and practice proper posture and to learn what the sweet spot feels like during the turn.

Never push/fire out of the barrel until you have allowed your horse to have his head back and he is headed away from the barrel in a straight line. Always be sure to tilt only your head and shoulders forward when you squeeze him with your heels, asking him to push/ fire out of the turn.

When doing this drill, you can make as many large circles as needed to make sure that your horse is working correctly before you tighten up the circle and push/fire out. But once you commit to tightening the circle, make only one medium circle before you start your approach to the barrel's check point and start your turn around the barrel.

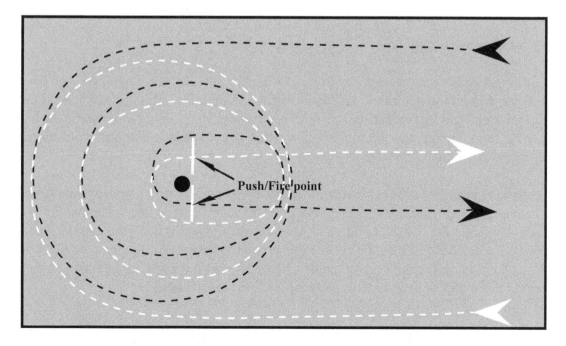

d.   Leg commands

Your legs play a huge part in barrel racing, since they give so many of the commands to your horse. Kicking your horse with your heels tells him to go, a single touch to his side tells him to move over, a squeeze with both heels tells him to increase his speed, the shift of your weight into the stirrups with forward motion tells him to rate, and your legs are your way of bracing yourself in the saddle against the g-forces you encounter when your horse rates a barrel.

From day one, everything we do when we are training a horse, teaches him to give to pressure. When we ask him to lead, we pull on the rope, and he gives to the pressure and moves toward you and away from the pressure. When we apply pressure with our rein to his neck, he turns, moving away from the rein pressure. When we pull back on the reins, putting pressure on his mouth, he stops his forward movement, again giving to the pressure.

Leg commands are just another tool in our toolbox for communicating with our horse when asking him to do something. Your horse already knows basic leg commands from his early training. When you apply leg pressure by kicking, your horse knows that you want him to move forward.

But in barrel racing, it is very important for a horse to know and understand much more detailed leg commands from the rider. He has to be able to maneuver around the barrels with accuracy, at high speeds, and respond instantly to just a touch of the rider's leg to his side when he is asked to move over just a few inches. Your horse needs to know that when you apply leg pressure to the front cinch area, you want him to move his front end over. When you apply leg pressure to the back cinch area, you are asking him to move his hind end over. He also needs to understand the difference in just moving over from leg pressure and changing leads from leg pressure.

Teaching your horse to move away from your leg pressure just takes time, and you have to work with him to get him to respond to light pressure. But a horse must understand and work off light leg pressure before he ever starts barrel training. Since your horse has learned from day one that he should move away from pressure, learning independent leg pressure commands comes easily to him.

When teaching your horse to move off leg pressure, try riding with your legs out of your stirrups, and push your stirrup fenders back so you have direct contact with your horse's body. By removing the stirrup fenders from between your leg and your horse's sides, your horse can feel and respond to the leg commands easier. I also recommend that you use a pair of bumper spurs on your boots when teaching your horse leg commands; they help to make the commands clear and more defined to the horse.

e. Teaching flying lead changes
(continuous poles for controlled speed and collection)

When teaching a horse to make flying lead changes, the horse needs to work collected at the poll and in a controlled gait (speed). Horses have to learn how to use their hind end to drive with, without using their front end to pull with, in order to be able to switch their lead on the fly to make flying lead changes.

I designed this exercise to allow the rider to keep continuous motion and keep the horse collected at a controlled speed at all times. This provides the best environment for the horse to learn how to do flying lead changes, and the poles give the horse a visual aid to help him understand what you are asking him to do. By adding the poles while teaching my horse to work in a collected gait at a controlled speed, I am able to teach the horse to make flying lead changes without losing his continuous motion.

When you set up the six poles, be sure to set them up twenty-one feet apart, just as you would for pole bending. This allows your horse enough room between the poles to take a full stride in each lead before having to change to the other lead. For this exercise, you can use anything—barrels, cones, etc. —but I prefer using poles because they force you to use proper body posture and stay set back in your saddle's seat so that you can avoid hitting the poles with your body. Poles are also a great visual aid for the horse; they help keep him from dropping his shoulder and leaning into the turns.

This exercise is easy on the horse, as it asks him to think, but only for a few moments, then he gets relief and can process what he has just done without becoming tired or burned out on the exercise.

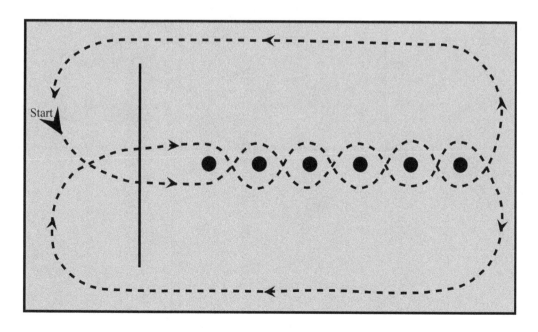

f. Pole bending and flying lead changes

Flying lead changes are important for all barrel horses to be comfortable with. I have found that one of the best tools for practicing flying lead changes is the pole bending pattern. Poles are a great way to avoid boredom when working your horse on flying lead changes, and your horse gets to learn another event to compete in.

It is important to place the poles exactly twenty-one feet apart when you set up the pole bending pattern, this allows your horse to have room for a complete stride between the poles in one lead before he has to change to the other lead.

Some people like to use a figure eight to teach their horses to make a flying lead change. While it works well, I find that horses get bored with it very fast.

1)   Large figure eight
2)   Pole-bending pattern

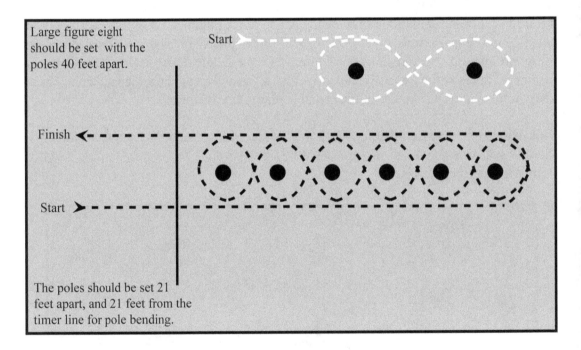

CORRECT BARREL TURNS

Correct barrel turns begin and end with balance, but you can't make a proper barrel turn if you don't give your horse the proper commands at the correct time. In order for your horse to make a correct barrel turn, he has to have his balance throughout the entire turn to keep from stalling out and losing precious time or hitting a barrel.

Checking: The horse has to be checked at the proper time to rate in the proper place to make a correct barrel turn.

Rating: Your horse has to rate his speed down by planting both of his hind feet in the correct place to slow down his forward motion, without stopping completely, to make a correct barrel turn.

Turning: Your horse also needs to be in the proper place to start his turn in order to make a correct barrel turn without losing his balance. Before you start the turn, the horse has to be finished rating his speed down.

One of the most common mistakes made by barrel racers is asking the horse to turn while he is still trying to rate his speed down. This causes the horse to lose his balance by trying to rate and turn at the same time. This also causes horses to slice and hit barrels by forcing the horse to drop his inside shoulder in order keep his balance so that he can make the turn.

Turning balance: Starts with proper rate that allows the horse to get both hind feet under him before he starts his turn. It is also very important for the rider to sit still and not shift his or her weight to one side or the other during the entire turn, as doing so can cause your horse to lose his balance. While we don't want to throw our horse off balance with our body position, we can use our weight to help our horse maintain his balance when needed.

Hand positioning: Is also very important for making a proper barrel turn. A horse needs to use his head and neck for balance, so it is very important not to take that away from him when you ask him to turn. We want to just tip our horse's nose to the inside of the turn, so he can follow his nose around the barrel without ever losing his balance.

a. Checking

There are three parts to checking a horse properly.

Your hands do the first part when you give a light tug and release on the reins to send a command to your horse. It is very important to release the pressure on the rein once you pull back enough for the bit to apply pressure to the horse's mouth. The release of the rein pressure on the horse's mouth is the end of the hand check command. The check command (pressure) has to start and stop for the horse to know that it is a command. If the command doesn't stop before the horse is asked to turn, the horse will start ignoring the hand check with the rein as a command to rate. Instead, he will start to relate the hand checking with the command to turn, causing major problems later on.

Bracing with your saddle horn is the second part of the hand check. Dropping your outside rein and pushing forward on the saddle horn with your outside hand immediately after you check the horse with your reins helps the rider brace for the horse's rate.

Your legs are the third and most important part of checking your horse. Your legs give the third part of the checking signal when you push your feet forward, shifting your weight to your stirrups, and sitting all the way back in your saddle's seat. Using your legs along with your reins makes it easier for the horse to understand the check command when you are teaching him how to rate.

The hand check and the dropping of the outside rein work like a warning signal to your horse that you want him to rate. There will be just the slightest moment between the hand check and the leg check, while you reach for the horn, before you can brace with your legs, but you need to get it all done before the horse collects and rates.

It is very important for you to complete all of the parts of the check command and bracing so that you are ready for the change of momentum when the horse does rate. If you don't use your legs to brace yourself when you check your horse, the change in the forward momentum will throw you up in the saddle, and you may just end up going over your horse's head.

b.   Rating

Teaching a horse to rate takes time and patience. Most horses have to learn how to rate, and the ones that already know how to rate something, like a cow, still need to learn how to rate when the rider asks them to, by giving them a signal. If we want our horses to rate when we ask them to rate—and not when they think they should rate—they need to learn the rider's signal for asking them to rate. In barrel racing, checking is the rider's signal for asking the horse to rate.

In order for a horse to rate his speed down from a wide-open run, he first has to collect and gain full control of his body. Once he has collected, he can then gather his hind end and plant both of his hind feet to rate and slow down his forward motion without stopping completely. A horse has to rate his speed down from a full-out run in order to keep his balance to make a proper turn around the barrel.

If the rider does not allow the horse to rate before he tries to turn the barrel, the horse will not be in control of his legs and he will lose his balance, making it impossible for the horse to make a proper controlled turn around the barrel.

It is also very dangerous for a horse to try to turn out of balance. If a horse is out of balance when he is asked to start his turn, he can only use one of his hind feet to rate. This usually causes him to stumble, overreach, or fall trying to get his balance to make the turn. Ensuring that your horse is able to rate the barrel in balance is not only for the horse's soundness and safety but also for the rider's.

Learning how to rate your horse properly is one of the hardest parts of barrel racing, and teaching your horse how to rate on command is one of the most important parts of barrel horse training. If your horse does not learn how to rate the barrel properly, you will never know your horse's full potential as a barrel horse. I felt the need to include a lot of exercises and detailed diagrams and instructions on how to teach a horse to rate a barrel properly in this book, as there is very little detailed explanation available on the subject.

c.   Turn and balance

It is vital for your horse to maintain his balance throughout his entire turn if he is going to make a proper barrel turn.

From the point where we check our horse to the point that we push/fire out of our turn, we need to stay out of our horse's way and in the center of his back until he has completed his entire turn and is ready to push/fire out of it.

Horses need the ability to use their heads to maintain their balance throughout their entire turn. When we take our horse's head away from him while he is trying to turn, by pulling too hard on our reins, he loses the ability to maintain his balance with his head and has to try to turn off balance, usually causing him to hit a barrel or blow out of his turn.

The rider's body position is also vital for the horse to successfully keep his balance throughout his turn; just the slightest shift of our weight can throw the horse off balance.

I like to use a stick horse drawing to show the correct body positioning at the different parts of the turn.

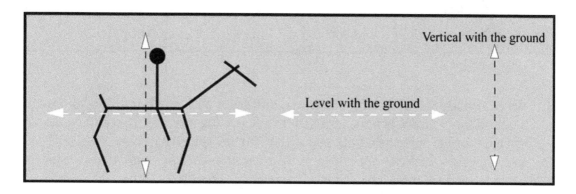

1.   **Vertical body position, level with the ground and the horse,** is used during your horse's entire barrel turn. This allows him to run and turn in four-wheel drive. Leaning too far forward takes away his power to push with his hind end, and leaning too far backward takes away his power to pull with his front end.

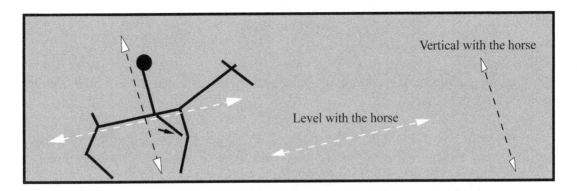

2. **Vertical body position with the horse and level with the horse** is used when the horse rates. This allows him to switch his balance to his rear end. The rider also needs to brace for the rate with his or her legs by pressing down and forward in the stirrups to maintain this body position.

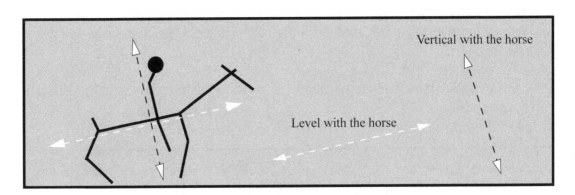

3. **Vertical body position with the horse and level with the horse** is also used at the push/fire point. When the horse starts to leave the turn, his front end comes up just a bit for the horse to start to pull with it, but the rider needs only to tilt his head and shoulders forward, not his entire body, to prevent drag and wind resistance. Leaning too far forward takes away the horse's power to push/fire out of the turn with his hind end. The rider needs to stay seated and vertical with the horse and not lean too far forward so that the horse can use both his front end and his hind end to leave the turn with the maximum amount of power.

d. Correct hand positioning for turns

Having your hands in the correct position to make a barrel turn is vital to the success of your turn. So before we go any further, I need to establish a few of the barrel racing terms that are used to help the rider to understand which hand we are talking about. In barrel racing, if the barrel is at your right foot or side, your right hand is your inside hand and your left hand is your outside hand.

So when we say inside hand, we mean the hand that is closest to the barrel that you are about to turn. When we say outside hand, we are referring to the hand that is farthest from the barrel.

Next, you need to find the correct spot on the reins for your hands so that you are ready to start the turn when you get to the barrel. Before you ever enter the arena, you should gather your reins to this point and be ready to start your run. This way, when you get to the first barrel, your hand will already be in the correct place on the reins for you to start your turn. Once you determine the correct spot on the reins for your hands, you can mark this spot with a piece of electrical tape so that you can feel the correct spot to slide your hands to on the reins without looking down. This also helps the rider to be consistent in using the same spot on the reins so that the horse gets the exact amount of rein pressure every time.

To find the correct hand spot on your reins for you and your horse, you need to make sure that you are sitting straight up in your saddle, with your arms stretched straight forward pointing to your horse's mouth. Then gather your reins on each side, to the point that there is no slack but you are not pulling on your horse's head. Your horse's head should be in a relaxed position, and you should be applying just enough pressure to the reins to remove any slack in the reins, but not enough pressure to causes him to give at the poll. This is your starting spot for your hands on the reins. Always make sure that each rein on both sides is collected the same amount; one rein should never be longer than the other.

We never want to take away our horse's balance by pulling on his head while he is trying to turn. When a horse's head is taken away by a rider trying to force the turn, he loses his ability to make a proper barrel turn. When we ask our horse to turn, we need to hold our hand forward, in a straight line to his mouth, making our arm an extension of the reins. We do not want to pull back, lift up, or pull down. We only want the horse's head to turn enough so that we can see the bulge of the horse's eye on the side of his face. While keeping our arm straight and pointing toward the horse's mouth, we can move our hand away from the horse's neck just enough, about four to six inches, to get him to release to the pressure and show us the tip of his nose and the bulge of his eye. A horse needs to use his head and neck for balance, so it is very important not to take that away from him.

Correct hand position for entering the barrel turn.

Correct hand position during the barrel turn.

Correct hand position leaving the barrel turn.

TEACHING THE PROPER BARREL TURN

(Be sure to measure and mark your pocket and pocket points when using this exercise.)

By teaching horses to make a proper barrel turn before they ever have to learn the actual barrel pattern, you avoid most of the problems and headaches caused by the horse's confusion as to what you expect of him. When your horse already knows how to make a proper barrel turn before you go to the arena, learning the actual barrel pattern is the easy part. And when the rider knows how to ride a proper barrel turn, he or she will be able to get on a finished barrel horse and ride him correctly and with ease.

Before you ever take a young horse to the arena and show him the barrel pattern, you need to teach him how to make a proper barrel turn first. And before you compete on a horse that has already been shown the barrel pattern, you need to make sure that he knows how to make a popper barrel turn. And before you get on a finished barrel horse that already knows how to make a proper barrel turn, you need to know how to ride a proper barrel turn.

By using this training technique to teach a proper barrel turn, you reduce your training time, eliminate burnout on the barrel pattern, and gain accuracy and consistency in your runs. This exercise is one of the best for teaching consistency in checking, rating, turning, and pushing/firing out of the barrel to both horse and rider at the same time.

It is vital for the rider to be as consistent as possible when doing this drill so that the horse and rider can get their timing together. This drill is also designed to teach the barrel turn in both directions and with continuous motion, like the barrel pattern, while giving the horse a longer break between barrel turns to digest what he has learned and relieves the pressure of having to make quick speed changes.

This exercise works exceptionally well because the horse has only one turn at a time to deal with. Then he gets a long break to think about what he was just asked to do before he has to try it again. This helps the horse stay relaxed and understand what he is being asked to do.

This exercise is designed to be done at just about any speed. Start out at a lope. If the horse doesn't rate correctly when doing this exercise the first time, just go on and try it again on the next turn. If the horse is still not rating, slow things down, go down to a trot, stop him at the rate point, back him up a step or two, and then go on and finish your turn.

Never correct your horse during this exercise. You never want to correct (get after, tune up, etc.) your horse while doing this exercise, as everything is all in the same place/spot, and that spot will start becoming a bad place/spot to be. As a result, this exercise won't work for that horse anymore.

a.   Marking the proper barrel turn exercise
(Step #1)

Now that you have learned how to measure your pockets and mark your pocket points and know where you need your horse to go in order to make a proper barrel turn, you can teach your horse where these points are with this exercise. This unique exercise teaches your horse where these points are while teaching you consistency and building your muscle memory. It allows you to make barrel turns over and over, and without burning your horse out on the barrel pattern.

You will need four ten or twelve-foot portable panels, one fifty-gallon barrel, and a bag of lime.

1) **Barrel placement:** Pick one of the long sides of the arena. Find the approximate center of the arena fence, draw a thirty-five- to forty-foot line with your stick in the dirt. Start at the center point of the arena fence and go toward the other side of the arena. Place your barrel on this line, twenty feet away from the fence.
2) **Panel placement:** Take two of your portable panels and place them in the shape of a V, along the same side of the arena. Then take your other two panels and do the same thing. There should be thirty feet along the fence, between each set of panels, or fifteen feet to the panel from the center point of the arena. The panels create a visual aid for the horse and decrease his options, making going around the barrels the easiest option.
3) **Mark the barrel center point:** Draw a line with a stick that crosses the center of your barrel from the arena end fence toward the opposite end fence of the arena. Your barrel should be sitting in the center of where your lines cross, twenty feet away from the side fence.

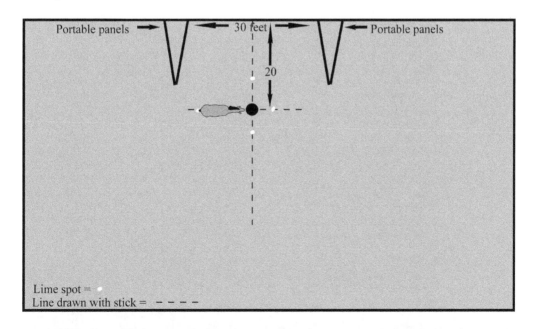

4) **Mark your barrel pocket:** Place your horse's nose on the outside edge of the barrel with his body parallel to the fence. Where his tail drops to the ground is your pocket start point #1.

5) **Mark the rest of your barrel points:** You mark the rest of this exercise just like you would when marking the barrel pattern (See: Marking the barrel pocket points in Chapter 3). Your point #2 is two-thirds of the distance of point #1, and points #3 and #4 are one-third of the distance of point #1.

6) **Now connect your points:** Start at point #1 and draw an arced line to points #2, #3, and #4, connecting your barrel points with a lime line. This is your barrel pocket.

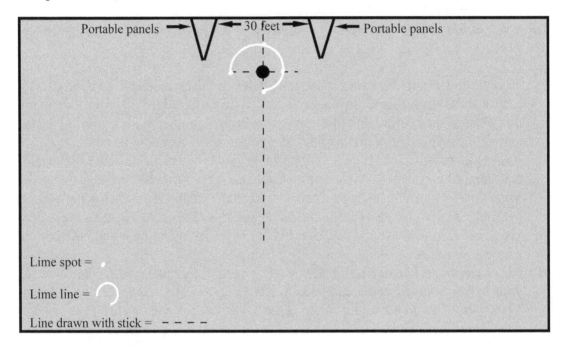

Marking the proper barrel turn exercise
(Step #2)

Now that you have your pocket points marked, you can mark the exercise entrance and exit points.

7) **Exercise Entrance Point:** Extend your pocket point #1 toward the opposite arena side fence, about forty feet. Mark the entire forty-foot line with your lime.

8) **Exercise Exit Point:** Take your lime and extend your pocket point #4 parallel with the arena side fence, about forty feet toward the arena end fence. Mark the entire forty-foot line with your lime.

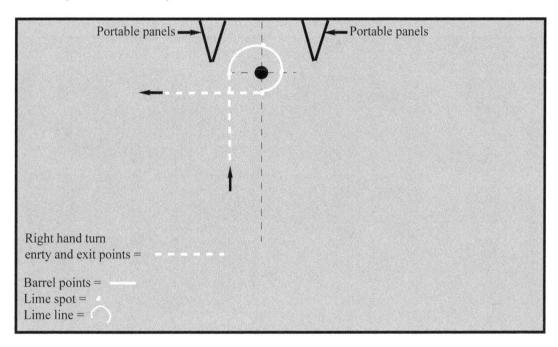

Once you have marked your exercise entry and exit points, you can mark your barrel points. (Check, rate, turn, and push/fire points.)

9) **Rate point:** Your rate point for this exercise is where your entry point line crosses your exit point line. You don't have to mark the rate point, as it is already marked by your entry and exit point lines.

10) **Check point:** The check point for this exercise is one of your horse's body lengths, from the tip of his nose to the point that his tail hits the ground.

11) **Turn point:** The measurement for the turn point for this exercise is also one of your horse's body lengths, from the tip of his nose to the point that his tail hits the ground.

12) **Push/fire point:** The push/fire point for this exercise is at your pocket point #4.

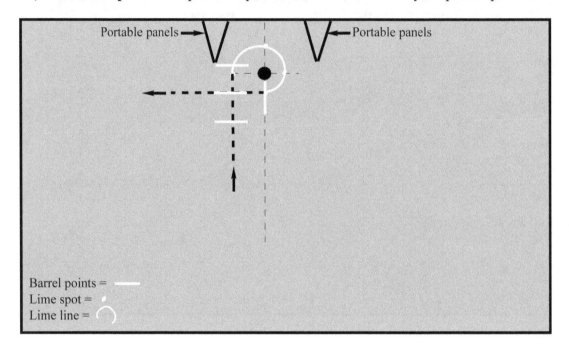

Marking the proper barrel turn exercise
(Step #3)

Now that we have the right-hand turn marked, we can mark the left-hand turn.

13) **Mark your barrel pocket** with your horse's nose in the center of the barrel and his body parallel to the fence. This is your pocket point #1. Mark the rest of your barrel points. Two-thirds of the distance of point #1 is your point #2, and one-third is your point #3 and #4.

14) **Exercise Entrance Point:** Extend your pocket point #1 toward the opposite arena side fence, about forty feet. Mark the entire forty-foot line with your lime.

15) **Exercise Exit Point:** Take your lime and extend your pocket point #4 parallel with the arena side fence, about forty feet toward the arena end fence. Mark the entire forty-foot line with your lime.

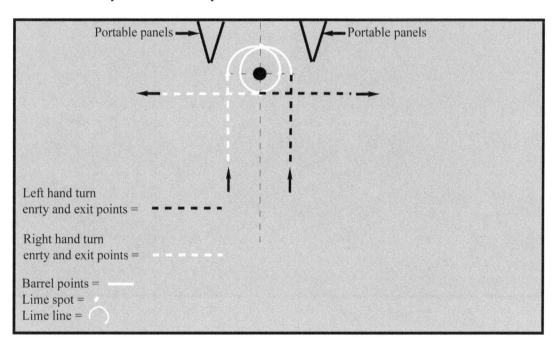

Once you have marked your exercise entry and exit points, you can mark your barrel points. (Check, rate, turn, and push/fire.)

16) **Your rate point:** For this exercise, the rate point is where your entry point line crosses your exit point line. You don't have to mark the rate point, as it is already marked by your entry and exit point lines.
17) **Your check point:** For this exercise, the check point is one of your horse's body lengths, from the tip of his nose to the point that his tail hits the ground.
18) **Your Turn point:** For this exercise, the turn point is also one of your horse's body lengths, from the tip of his nose to the point that his tail hits the ground.
19) **Your push/fire point:** For this exercise, the push fire/point is at your #4 pocket point

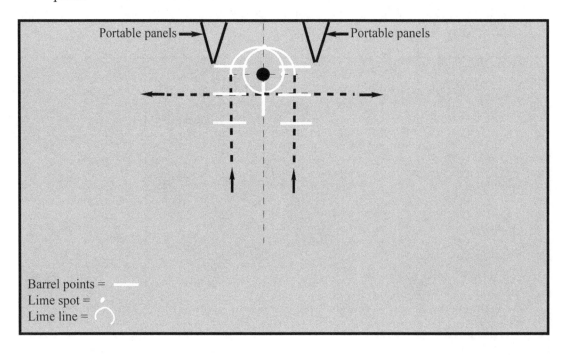

b. Proper barrel turn exercise
(right turn)

Now that you have marked your pocket points, barrel points, and entrance and exit points, you can start the proper barrel turn exercise. As with all the exercises in this book, it needs to be repeated at least five times for a horse to learn how to do everything correctly.

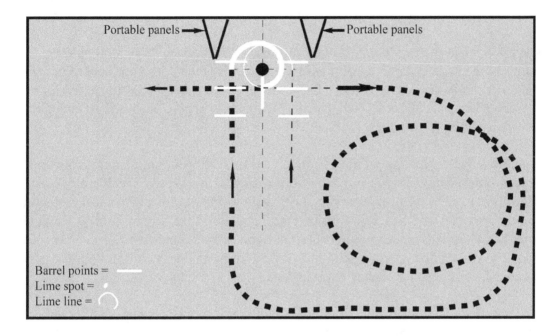

Start on the right side of the arena, ask your horse to pick up his inside lead (right lead), and lope a large circle. Make sure that your horse stays in the correct lead; you can make as many large circles as you need to get your horse working in a nice collected controlled lope. Once you reach the arena centerline, turn and make a straight approach to your marked barrel. Be sure to keep your approach straight to ensure that you are entering the exercise at the correct angle.

You should be in a slow lope when your horse's front feet reach the check point. Check your horse, drop your outside rein, and push back on your horn while putting your weight in your stirrups and pushing your feet forward.

Remember to make sure that there is a definite change in the horse's approach speed (gait) to his turning speed (gait). If the difference is not very noticeable when we do the training exercises at slower speeds, then when we ask our horse to make a fast run on the exercise, our horse will try to run through his turns and not rate his speed (gait) down for them. The approach speed needs to always be faster than the turn speed, or your horse will think that he needs to be going the same speed around the barrel as he is when he is approaching it, and he will never learn how to rate properly.

You want your horse to stop at the rate point. If he does not, back him up until his front feet are at the rate point, stop him there, and pat his neck so he knows this is where you want him to rate. Wait for about ten seconds, so he knows that you meant for him to stop there.

Then ask your horse to move straight forward at a walk until his front feet are at your turn point. Be sure that you don't shift your weight. Stay seated in the center of your horse and keep your feet forward in your stirrups.

When you reach the turn point, bring your inside foot back to its natural position and apply just the slightest amount of pressure to the cinch area with your heel to get your horse to bend his ribcage. At the same time, move your hand toward the barrel and away from his neck, about six to ten inches, asking him to give his head just enough for you to see the bulge of his eye.

Continue to guide him around the barrel on your marked path, until his front feet reach the push/fire point, and release the pressure with your heel to the cinch area. As soon as the horse reaches the push/fire point, bring your hand back toward his neck, releasing the rein pressure, and squeeze both of your heels into him, asking him to leave the barrel at a lope. This is a continuous motion exercise so that when you leave the right-hand turn, you will be set up to start the left-hand turn. That way, you just need to make sure to ask your horse to change leads and start your left-hand circle.

Repeat the exercise at least five times in each direction at the same speed. If your horse is doing everything correctly, you can speed up the exercise on the next day. You do not want to burn your horse out. When you come back on the next day, he will pick up right where you left off. I don't like to do this exercise any more than five times in each direction in a day.

If at any time the horse is not doing every part of the exercise correctly, do not speed it up until he is doing every part of the turn correctly—except for the following reason.

This exercise's main function is to teach your horse how to rate. If your horse is not rating down after the first five times you take him through it, then you need to force him to rate. I don't like to have to force a horse to rate, but if he just doesn't get it, then you have to let him figure it out on his own.

First, lope your circle until you get to the approach point at the arena halfway point. Then, instead of loping up to the turn slowly, run your horse in hard and fast up to the check point, check him hard, and even if he doesn't rate down his speed when he gets to the turn point, ask him to turn. With this exercise, he has no other option than to turn the barrel or hit the fence. Believe me, he will turn the barrel. You may have to do this several times until he figures out for himself that it is easier to rate his speed down and make the turn correctly than try to make the turn at full speed.

You can see on the diagram that the right-hand turn starts and goes directly into a large right-hand circle before the horse ever approaches the right barrel turn. This allows the rider to take the time to get the horse in the proper lead and working at a nice controlled gait before he ever approaches the turn. The rider can make several circles if needed to get the horse to pay attention, pick up the correct lead, or settle down before he starts the actual turning exercise.

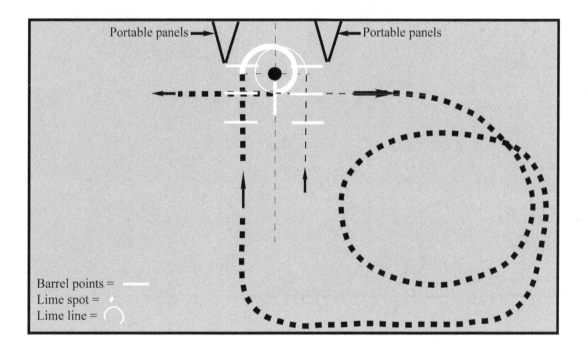

c.   Proper barrel turn exercise
(left turn)

Now that you have done your first right turn, it is time to do a left turn. This is a continuous motion exercise, so you go straight into the second step as soon as you leave the exit point of the barrel. Be sure to repeat the exercise at least five times in each direction for your horse to learn how to do everything correctly.

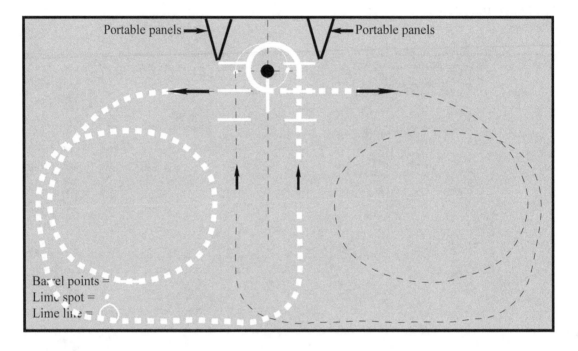

Your horse needs to pick up his left lead once he leaves the exit point. If he did not pick it up when he was asked to leave, then you need to ask him to change leads before you get to the arena corner. Lope a large circle on the left side of the arena, making sure that he is in the correct lead (left lead) and working in a nice controlled gait.

Once you reach the arena centerline, turn and make a straight approach to your marked barrel. Be sure to keep your approach straight to ensure that you are entering the exercise at the correct angle.

You should be in a slow lope when your horse's front feet reach the check point. Check your horse, drop your outside rein, and push back on your horn while putting your weight in your stirrups and pushing your feet forward.

You want your horse to stop at the rate point. If he does not, back him up until his front feet are at the rate point. Stop him there and pat his neck so that he knows this is where you want him to stop. Wait for about ten seconds so he knows that you meant for him to stop here.

Then ask your horse to move straight forward at a walk until his front feet are at your turn point. Be sure that you don't shift your weight. Stay seated in the center of your horse and keep your feet forward in your stirrups.

When you reach the turn point, bring your inside foot back to its natural position and apply just the slightest amount of pressure to the cinch area with your heel to get your horse to bend his ribcage. At the same time, move your hand toward the barrel and away from his neck, about six to ten inches, asking him to give his head just enough for you to see the bulge of his eye.

Continue to guide him around the barrel on your marked path until his front feet reach the push/fire point; then release the pressure with your heel to the cinch area.

As soon as he reaches the push/fire point, bring your hand back toward his neck, releasing the rein pressure, and squeeze both of your heels into him, asking him to leave the barrel at a lope. You will be set up to go back and do another right-hand turn.

Continue this exercise in both directions at a lope until you and your horse have all of the points down and your horse changes his speed at the proper rate point every time before you add any more speed. This exercise can be done at a full-out run, just like in a barrel race if needed. Try not to overdo it on this exercise, or your horse will start to resent the exercise and you will lose it as a training tool. Save the hard fast runs for the barrel pattern.

This exercise helps both the horse and the rider to work on consistency with commands and responses while building muscle memory, so be sure that you are conscious of the commands you are giving and that you are being consistent. This exercise is a great tool for the rider to practice his or her commands without burning the horse out.

d.   Proper barrel turn exercise
(adding speed)

Keep in mind that a horse's gait starts at a walk, then to a trot, a slow lope, a high lope, a run, and then a high-speed run. **For this exercise only, we need to make sure that there are two gait (speed) changes from the approach gait (speed) to the turn gait (speed), until our horse has every part the exercise down and is doing it all correctly.** Then we can go to one gait change between the approach speed and turn speed, like in an actual barrel racing run, where there is only one gait change from the approach speed to the turn speed.

Once you have taken your horse through the exercise in both directions at a lope to the rate point, and a walk throughout the turn, and he has seen what you want him to do and where you want him to go, you can start adding speed. Remember that this exercise needs to be repeated at least five times, in each direction, for your horse to learn how to do everything correctly and on both sides.

When we add speed to this exercise, we need to remember to make sure that there is a definite change in the horse's approach speed (gait) and his turning speed (gait). If we don't make the difference very noticeable when we are doing the training exercises at slower speeds, then when we ask our horse to make a faster run on the barrel pattern, our horse will try to run through his turns and not rate his speed (gait) down for them.

So when adding speed to this training exercise, we want to increase our approach speed but keep our turn speed two gaits slower. So if your approach speed is a run, then your turn speed should be a slow lope. Make sure that your horse can correctly do at least five right and five left turns at this speed before you add any more speed.

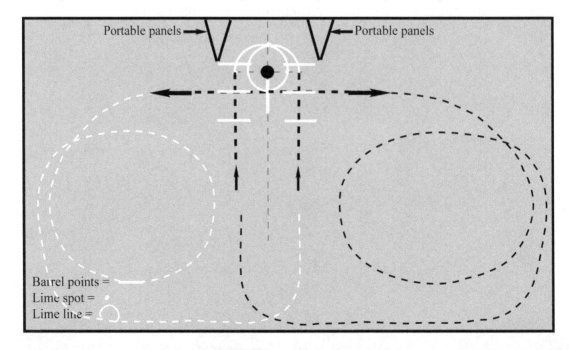

EXERCISES FOR PRACTICING
CONSISTENT RATE AND TURN

All the exercises in this book need to be repeated at least five times for the horse to understand them and learn how to do everything correctly. You should do all exercises at a walk the first few times, then at a trot, until the horse is changing his speed and rating the barrel every time.

Once your horse understands the exercise and is doing it correctly every time, you can move the speed up to a lope. When the horse starts rating the barrel consistently at that speed, you can move up to a run. While you can do these exercises over and over, it is important not to overdo any of them. These exercises, like all exercises, should not be overdone. Once that happens, they lose their effectiveness as a training tool.

A horse's gait (speed) goes from a stop to a walk, then to a trot, slow lope, high lope, run, and then a high-speed run. When teaching a horse to rate something, we need to make sure that there are two gait (speed) changes from the approach gait (speed) to the turn gait (speed). We want to over exaggerate the gate (speed) difference to our horse.

For all rate training exercises, you need two gait changes from your approach speed to your turn speed. **Use two gait speed changes only in training, not in competition.**

For actual barrel racing runs, there is only one gait change, from the approach speed to the turn speed.

These rate training exercises are excellent for helping finished horses and riders work on their timing with each other. These exercises are also great for teaching young horses how to make a complete barrel turn and learn how to rate properly and get their butt underneath them to make a correct barrel turn. All of these exercises also help both horse and rider work on their timing with each other without burning the horse out on the barrel pattern.

a. Rate and turns
(rollback turns for barrel horses)

I am not a big fan of rollback turns for teaching barrel horses how to turn a barrel. Not only do they cause a horse to stall out and lose his continuous motion in order to do them properly, they also cause your horse to start hitting barrels. A complete circle turn is much faster than a rollback turn since your horse doesn't lose his momentum. A horse needs to set both hind feet when he rates to make a complete balanced circle turn without stalling out. A rollback turn or pivot turn will cause a horse to hit barrels in barrel racing.

I like to do this exercise to teach a barrel horse to turn. It works like the rollback, but it helps keep the horse from stalling out and allows him to practice his turns the way he needs to in a barrel race.

However, I do feel that rollbacks have their place in barrel horse training, but they are not good for teaching barrel turns. Rollbacks are a great starting point for training young horses that don't know anything. They help teach horses to collect and set one hind foot underneath them to pivot on for a rollback turn. All of these rollback exercises should be done at a slow trot or walk, two or three times, before you ever do them at a lope or run. This will show the horse what you expect from him, keeping him calm and willing to run up to a wall, fence, or corner. **No surprises.** This exercise will also help build trust with your horse. He will learn to trust you to turn him out of the wall, corner, or fence. Without that trust, you might as well go home.

This exercise can be done anywhere, with or without barrels, but the visual aid of a barrel helps increase the learn-ability of the exercise. The fence corner is also a visual aid to help the horse understand where you want him to go. Since it reduces his options, it makes it easier for him to understand what you are asking him to do. Once your horse has the concept, you can do this exercise anywhere without the visual aids.

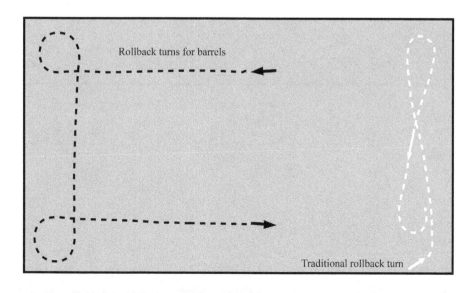

Rollback turns for barrels

Traditional rollback turn

b.   Teaching rate on the barrel

It helps most horses to have a barrel as a visual aid to learn how to collect and rate properly for a barrel turn. This exercise works great to teach them that they have to rate their speed down to make the turn.

This exercise also works great on horses that have natural rate, allowing you to push them up into the pocket without pushing them by the barrel.

For a chargy horse: Set the barrel only fifteen feet from the arena fence corner.

For a natural rated horse: Move the barrel out five feet farther from the fence than you would for a chargy horse.

Always do these exercises at a walk and trot before you ever run your horse on them.

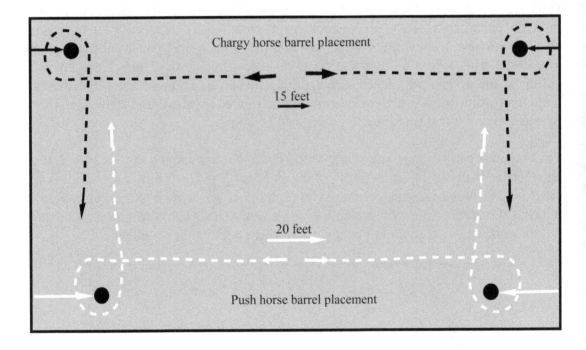

c. Continuous barrels for right and left barrel turns

This exercise is extremely helpful for letting your horse practice collecting and rating the barrels. The corner of the fence frames the barrel for a visual aid, which leaves the horse only one option for keeping his forward motion. The fence also helps him to make a complete turn before he tries to leave. The visual aid of the fence corners helps your horse to have a clear understanding of what you are asking from him.

This exercise, like all exercises, should be done at a slow pace before you ever go fast so that you don't break your horse's trust. Walk your horse through the turns first, and then trot through the turns before you ever make a run through them. Your horse needs to first see what you want him to do so that he will learn to trust you when you run him into the corner. Once he knows that he can trust that you will not run him into the fence, you can add more speed to the exercise, and he will wait for you to give him the command before he starts his turn. Once again, trust is the key to this exercise. Don't break your horse's trust on this exercise, or he will start anticipating the turns and you will lose the power of control.

This exercise is a great way to increase your muscle memory away from the barrel pattern, so always be sure to use your check point when you check your horse and wait to turn until your horse gets to the turn point. This will make your commands become a natural reaction and increase your consistency.

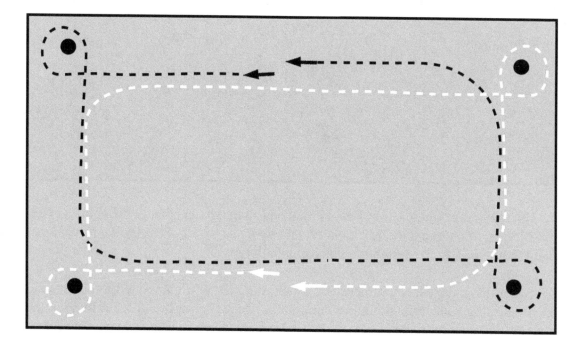

d.   Invisible barrel turns and trust

Once you've taught your horse how to make a proper barrel turn, it's time to make sure he completely understands what he has learned and is not relying on visual aids. This exercise gets our horse to do a correct barrel turn and learn to trust his rider's commands so he doesn't have to anticipate when to turn.

Always start slow and move your speed up as you go. Start your turns in one direction, then make the next turn to the opposite direction. Then do another to that direction and keep switching it up on him so that there is no pattern to your choice of direction and he has to rely on paying attention to you to know what direction you want to go next. Pretty soon, he will be working in a very controlled lope, waiting and listening for the next command and responding to the slightest of moves from you. Always check your horse and let him rate before you ask him to turn.

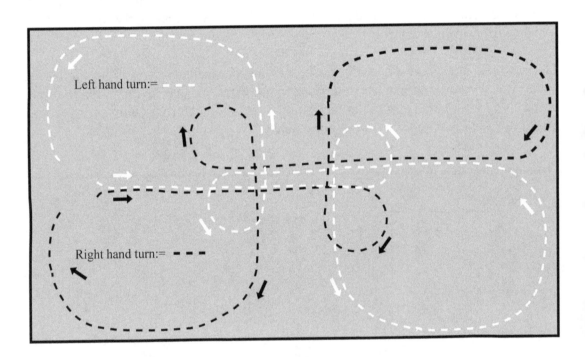

Left hand turn:= – – –

Right hand turn:= ▬ ▬ ▬

Be very consistent and clear in your commands so that he gets the same signals every time you ask him for a turn. And always make sure that your horse is going in a straight line for at least four strides before you ask him to turn.

Also, always make sure that there is enough room to do a complete barrel turn and leave finishing your turn without running into a fence. Try not to do your turns in the shape of the pattern to make sure he is listening to you and not just turning where he thinks there should be a barrel. Never let the horse anticipate and turn without you giving him the command to do so.

Once you feel that your horse is listening to you and waiting for your commands to make his turn, try checking to see if your horse trusts you enough to wait for your commands when you run the barrel pattern without any barrels. Your horse will have to wait for your commands since there is no visual aid from the barrel; if he trusts you enough to wait for you to give him the command to turn, he will have no problems making a perfect run without any barrels.

HOW TO USE THE MARKED
BARREL PATTERN

(for fine-tuning or starting barrel horses)

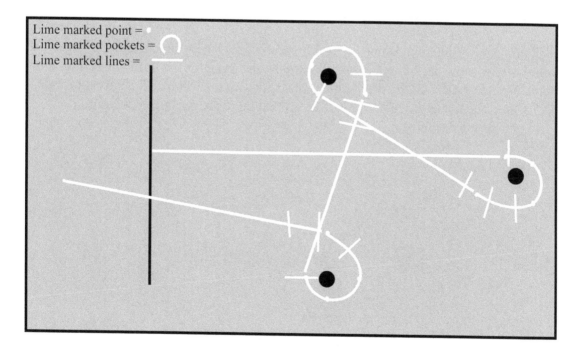

Lime marked point =
Lime marked pockets =
Lime marked lines =

Once you have your barrel pattern marked with your lime, you are ready to make a training run. Walk your horse through the pattern on the chalk lines. When you get to the check point, check your horse; he should stop with his front feet on the check line. Look around you; make sure that you can see the lime lines and points easily. If you are not able to see all of them easily, stop and fix them so that you can easily see them from your horse's back.

Remember to always use the correct body posture. Ask your horse to continue, drop your outside rein, but keep going straight to the turn point. When you get to the turn point, press you're inside heel into the horse's cinch area lightly so he will bend his ribcage. Then move your inside rein six to ten inches toward the barrel. Do not lift, pull back, or pull down on the rein. Move it away from your horse's neck toward the barrel, just enough to get your horse to give his nose and start to turn.

Follow the lime line around the barrel to the push/fire point. When you get to the push/fire point, you need to quickly move your hand back to your horse's neck, releasing the pressure on the reins and allowing him to straighten out his neck. Squeeze with both legs and ask him to move away from the barrel at a trot.

Pick up your outside rein, and when you get to the center point between the first and second barrel, pull him up to a walk again. Continue to the second barrel. It will be the same as the first barrel. Check, drop your outside rein, move forward to the turn point, and move your inside rein toward the barrel, asking your horse to turn and follow the lime line to the push/fire point. Quickly move your hand back toward the horse's neck and squeeze with both heels, asking your horse to leave at a trot.

Pick up your outside rein. When you get to the center of the second and third barrel, ask your horse to slow back down to a walk. Repeat the same for the third barrel, but make him continue at a trot all the way home. This helps you to visualize the barrel points and also allows the horse to see the lime lines so that there are no surprises for him.

a.   Correcting problems by reading your tracks

In this section, I have outlined the most common reasons for your tracks not being on the lime lines, but there are way too many to list them all. The most important thing to remember and to be aware of is the position of our body, hands, legs, and our weight movement at all times. Your horse can tell even the slightest difference in your movements. The commands that we give to our horse from his back have to be felt to be understood. The horse has to feel them because he can't see what we are doing up there. He has to be aware of every move we make and determine if it requires a response. Since everything we do while we are on his back affects his balance, it is also very important not to make any unnecessary movements. We don't want to confuse him by making any unnecessary movements that might be misunderstood as commands. Our horses need to be able to concentrate on the actual movements that are meant to be commands.

It is important to remember when reading your tracks that your horse is not trying to do the wrong thing. He is just trying to decipher your movements into commands and do what he thinks he is being asked to do. If your tracks are not where they should be, it is usually the rider who is not giving clear enough signals or is giving too many signals for the horse to follow; that causes the problem.

The rider is usually not even aware of it when he or she starts leaning, but the horse is always aware of the rider's movement because they can cause the horse to lose his balance. So if the rider starts leaning, the horse starts thinking the leaning is a command, and when he feels the rider lean, he moves to correct his balance. The riders' movement or leaning shows up when you look at your tracks and see that your horse is not going where you want him to. You can tell the rider was leaning if the horse's tracks are going along just fine on the line, and then suddenly leave the line and move off the line in one direction or another—but just off the line by a few feet—and then go back when the rider moved the horse back onto the line.

Videotape is also a great way of determining if the rider is the cause of the problem. Have someone videotape you from the back while you are running to a barrel. You can see the horse move in or out, depending on which way your body leans. It looks like the horse is just moving for no reason, until you watch the tape in super slow motion. Look at the run frame by frame and you will see that the rider leans first, then the horse moves to compensate for the movement. Videotape is another great tool for determining what went wrong with your run. When we watch the video tape and see the horse make a wrong movement, we need to look for the cause of the wrong movement. It is usually the rider who has done something to cause the horse to move. If not, it is usually the ground or something else, but it is rarely the horse, if he has been trained properly and knows where he is supposed to go.

When it is the horse that is causing the problem—like anticipating and doing his own thing—the problem is usually caused by the horse not having enough trust in his rider's ability to give proper, accurate, and consistent commands. This lack of trust causes the horse to have to rely on his own instincts at the last minute to decide when and where to stop and turn, making the horse nervous and anxious about running the barrels or even going into the arena. If you are not able to see anything that would have caused the horse to make the wrong movement, he may have a lameness problem and should be checked out.

All barrel horses need to get their adrenalin up before they make a barrel run, and if the horse has trust in his rider, he will get excited at the gate and his adrenalin will be up. He will not be scared to go into the arena since he knows what to expect and when to expect it. This is just one more reason to never break your horse's trust. So be sure not to get after your horse when he doesn't do what you are asking him to, until you have determined the reason why he didn't do it.

b.   Making your first run on the marked barrel pattern

Now that you have walked your horse through the marked barrel pattern, you are ready to make a run. Make sure that you have taken your horse through the "correct barrel turn" exercise at a run before you make a run on the barrel pattern. This helps both you and your horse to get ready for the actual marked barrel pattern. Always make sure that you have raked out any old tracks from the barrel pattern before you make this run, as you want to look at your tracks when you are done to see how you and your horse did.

Make sure you are ready in your mind. Gather your reins to their correct spot, be sure to use your body posture, and make a run. Don't hold back. Make a run like there is money on the line. You need to run hard and at full speed or your horse's tracks will be misleading.

The first run will probably be a bit awkward, with you trying to remember everything and do everything right at the right places. This is fine. Don't worry about any mistakes you make, and continue with your run until you are back across the timer line. It is important not to stop in the middle to fix any mistakes or pull up before you finish your run. We want to instill in our horse's mind that once he starts a barrel run, he has to finish it all the way before he can stop.

Now we can go back, look at our tracks, and see what part of the pattern we need to work on, and whether our horse is rating at the correct spot and with both hind feet. We can also see if he is waiting to start his turn and is turning at the correct spot.

If your horse has already run barrels before you started using this book and a marked barrel pattern, he may try to go back to his old habits. This is where we see if he has learned how to make a proper barrel turn.

If you have any old bad riding habits from your previous barrel racing, this is also where they will show up. We need to make sure to catch them now and correct them, so they don't cause problems later.

And if you are starting a young horse, this is where you can check to see whether he is ready for competition.

c. Reading your tracks
(rate and push/fire points)

Always make sure that you have raked out any old tracks before you make a new run on the marked barrel pattern. You need to be able to determine if you fixed the problem when you make a new run. If you can't determine which tracks are the new ones, you won't be able to tell if you fixed the problem or not. Your tracks will tell you if you are not running in the correct place when they are not on the lime line, but they will also tell you whether you are giving the correct commands at the correct time and place. All of your tracks can be right on the lime line, but that does not necessarily mean that your run was correct. There are several things that can still be wrong, and they will cost you time on your run, even if your tracks are on the lime line.

1) **The Rate point:** Your tracks can all be on the lime line, but if you are not checking your horse at the correct time, he may not be rating at the correct time, and this can cost you time on your run. When looking at your tracks, make sure that your skid marks (elevens) end on your rate point. If they do not, you will need to adjust your check point to correct this problem.

2) **The Push/Fire point:** Your tracks can all be on the lime line, but if your horse is not pushing/firing at the correct time, you are losing valuable time. When looking at your tracks you can tell if your horse pushed off hard at the correct point if there are deep dig marks at your push/fire point. If the deep dig marks are after your push/fire point, your horse is pushing/firing late, and this costs you valuable time. If there are no deep dig marks at your push /fire line, your horse is not pushing/firing hard out of the barrel. In order to make your horse push/fire hard when you ask him to at the push fire point, you have to squeeze with both heels at the same time. If he still does not push/fire hard out of the barrel, put some spurs on, and he will.

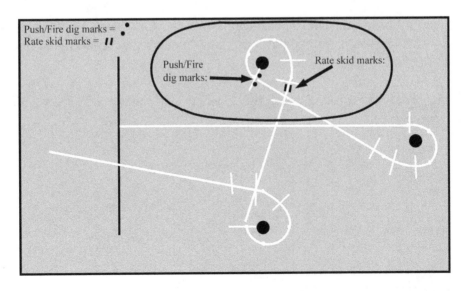

d.   Reading your tracks
(approaching and leaving the pockets)

1) **Pushing/Firing before the push/fire point:** Asking your horse to push/fire too soon will cause your horse to have to push/fire before he is done turning, while his ribcage is still bent in an arc, and he will float out away from the barrel. If you push/fire at the correct time, you will be lined up in a straight line to the next barrel and should only have to squeeze with both heels at the same time to get your horse to push/fire and make a straight line to the next barrel. By waiting to push fire until the push/fire point, your horse will have finished the turn and won't be thrown off balance and forced to lean and throw you out of balance.

2) **Not staying seated in the center of your horse:** Incorrect body posture is the number one cause for horses not staying in a straight line when they approach the barrel. Riders tend to lean when they are approaching or leaving a barrel. This causes the horse to have to move to get under the rider and compensate for the rider's weight change to keep his balance.

3) **Not continuing to use even leg pressure:** When asking the horse to push/fire out of his turn and run to the next barrel, you need to help guide your horse with your legs by applying even leg pressure or even kicks to keep him in a straight line. Once your horse has learned the barrel pattern, he usually knows where he should be going, but with young horses, you have to make sure to keep them in a straight line by using your legs to guide them.

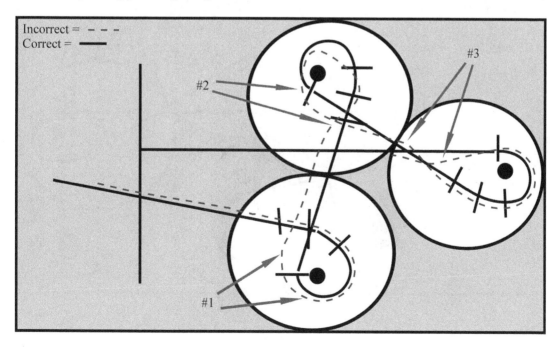

e.   Reading your tracks
(at the barrel pockets)

1) **Not turning your horse at the correct turn point:** If you don't wait until your horse has finished rating and ask him to turn and use your reins to start his turn before the turn point, you will cause your horse to drop into the barrel. If he manages to get by the barrel, he will have to bow out of the back side of the turn to keep his balance.

2) **Not collecting and rating properly:** If you don't check your horse at the correct check point and brace with your legs, your horse won't rate correctly at the rate point and he will have to try to turn on his front end, throwing you forward and causing him to go past the barrel. Your horse will then usually try to do a rollback turn to get back to the barrel, and most of the time, he will hit it. If he doesn't hit it, he will have to bow out the back side of the turn to get back into position. Rollback turns usually result in a hit barrel.

3) **Taking your horse's head away from him:** If you don't let your horse have his head to keep his balance, and you jerk it away from him during his turn, he will have to drop his shoulder into the barrel to keep his balance. This usually results in a hit barrel. If it doesn't, it always causes the horse to bow out the back side of the barrel to get around it.

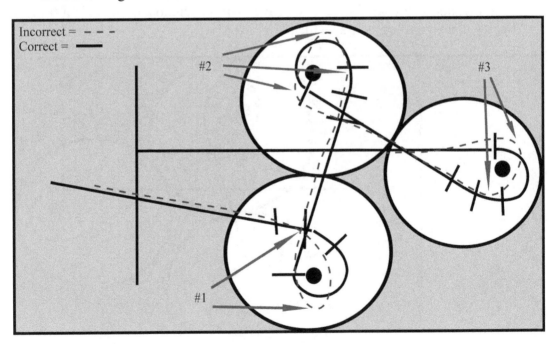

f.   Reading your tracks
(correcting problems)

The most costly and most often made mistakes are not running straight lines to your barrels, between your barrels, and on the run home.

1) **Not running directly to your first pocket point** causes your horse to make too large of a pocket and changes the entry point of the turn. This not only adds time to your run but also causes your horse to stop rating the barrel. This also causes your horse to have to do a rollback turn, which causes him to stall out and lose his forward momentum.

2) **Running straight to the barrel and then moving your horse over** to start your barrel pocket not only adds time to your run but also encourages your horse to turn in front of the barrel and head for home.

3) **Not leaving your turn off the second barrel in a straight line** to your third barrel pocket. This causes you to come into the third barrel at an arc, and most horses will not rate from this position. This will also cause your horse to start his turn too soon when he tries to get back in position to turn the barrel, and he will drop his inside shoulder. When your horse does not rate properly, he has to try to turn on its front end and ends up bowing out the back side of the turn and coming off the barrel wide.

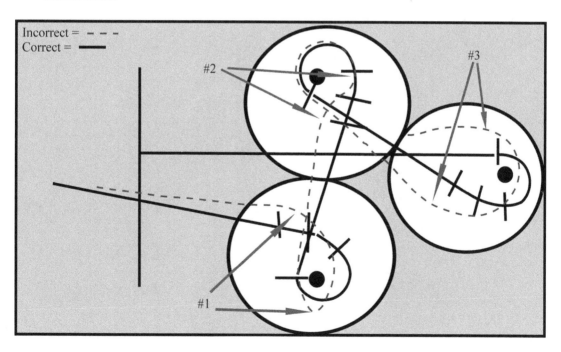

COMPETITION

a.   Entering the arena gates and alleys

Most arenas have a center alley, and the barrel pattern is set up to be in line with the center alley to be fair to all of the competitors. But you will come across some arenas that have an offset gate that favors a right-hand turn, or a left-hand turn for the first barrel. Many barrel races are won or lost by the arena gate setup. You need to be prepared to enter an arena at any gate point and be able to line your horse up at the optimal barrel pattern entry point. Just because the gate's entry point favors one side or the other, you don't have to give the competition the advantage.

The shut down area on the barrel pattern is never supposed to be less than forty-five feet, which is plenty of room for you to get your horse up to speed before he crosses the timer line. Always be sure to get your horse lined up in the center of the pattern (see: barrel pattern entry point) before you start your run, and don't let the pressure of the gate man or the competition force you to start your run until you are ready. You paid your entry fee just like everyone else, and you have the right to set up your run.

Make sure not to let your horse turn in a full circle when entering the arena, as you may get disqualified. Always keep forward motion. You can side pass but not make a complete turn. Barrel races are more lenient than rodeos on this rule, but it is just good practice to never allow your horse to turn in a full circle once he has entered the arena gate.

It is important for your horse to practice with all of the different entry gate points before you get to a barrel race or rodeo and have to make your run. Remember that your horse needs to have total trust in his rider. When your horse gets his adrenalin up and is ready to enter the arena gate, he needs to know exactly what to expect. If he hasn't learned that all gates are not lined up with the barrel pattern, he will take off from the wrong point and be out of position for the first barrel turn.

If the entry gate is in the center of the arena and is lined up with the barrel pattern, I don't worry too much about getting my horse into the arena to show him the gate. But if there is a side, or offset gate, I like to get my horse into the arena before he has to make a run in it. I like to show him the gate that he will use to come into the arena and line him up at the correct entry point for the pattern. This is always done at a slow walk so he can look at the arena and see everything while he is relaxed. Then when I get his adrenalin up to make my run there are no surprises. If I am not able to get in the arena before my run, I never run in the gate or alley. I let my horse come in nice and easy and never let him start to run until I am lined up with the barrel pattern at the correct entry point.

I like to use my exhibition time to teach my young horses about different entry gate positions. This is a great time and place to teach them to enter the arena and wait to start their run until they are lined up at the correct entry point. This also helps them learn to relax at the gate and get focused before they start their run. Even if there is a center gate, I like to walk them to the arena corner, as if it is the entry gate, and then walk them back over to the pattern entry point before I let them make a run. This also helps teach them that they need to wait until I ask before they start their run, which allows me to enter an arena gate without them taking off before I am ready. This also prepares them for future runs at arenas that don't have center entry gates so there are no unnecessary surprises.

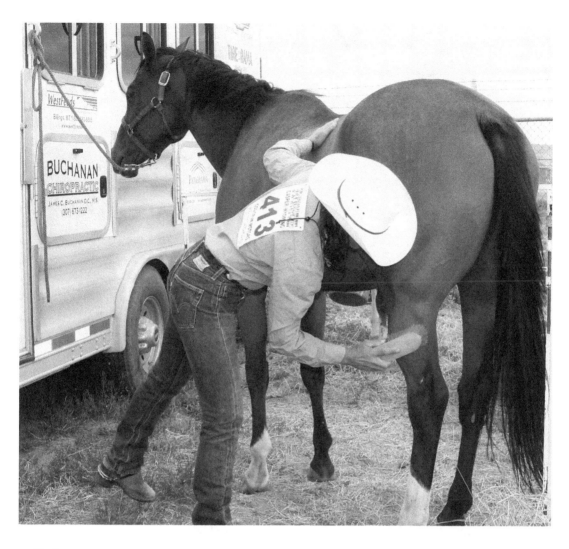

**Before you saddle your horse take the time to go over him with a brush from
head to toe, to check and make sure that he is ok before your run.**

Always use protective wraps on your horses' legs, and re-check them before your run.

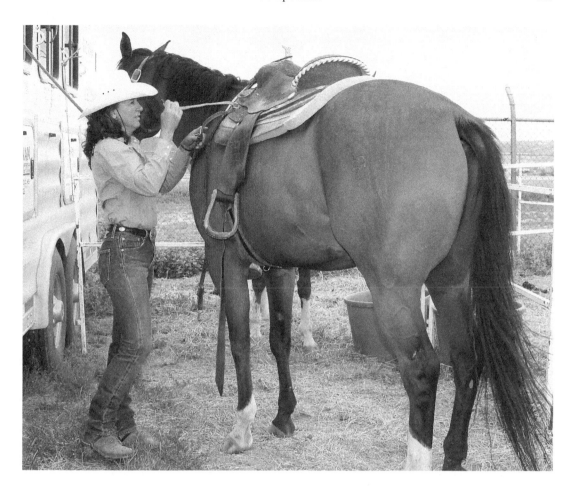

**Take the time before your run to check your tack for any
last minute problems or needed changes.**

b.   Rodeo's vs. barrel races

While the basics of barrel racing are the same for both rodeo and open barrel races, the rules are often very different. Before you enter a rodeo, be sure to read a copy of the rules. Most open armature rodeos and professional rodeos follow the WPRA (Women's Professional Rodeo) rulebook for barrel racing. There are many things that you are allowed to do at an open barrel race that you are not allowed to do at a rodeo. Failure to adhere to the rules results in disqualification, and ignorance of the rules is not an acceptable reason to overturn a disqualification and can cost you your winnings.

Your horse may be a seasoned barrel horse and broke for open barrel races, but if he has never competed at a rodeo, there are a lot of new things he will need to learn to deal with before he is rodeo broke. The best way to get your horse rodeo broke is to take him to some small armature rodeos first, and slowly get him accustomed to all of the different things, and then move him up to the larger rodeos. This will save you and your horse a lot of stress and a lot of wasted entry fees.

With rodeo, the payout is always better than with the open barrel races, as rodeos pay only the fastest top horses and don't break it down into divisions. In barrel racing, they break the payoff out into several divisions, paying out the top horses in three to six different divisions, diluting the payout to a minimal amount.

I have listed some of the most common things that your horse will need to become accustomed to if you want to compete in a rodeo.

Livestock: Some horses have never been around rough stock (bulls and bucking horses), and when they see them bucking around the arena, it spooks them and they won't want to go into the arena.

Entertainment: Clown acts usually have some kind of explosion as part of the act. It scares horses, and they won't want to go into the arena after hearing the explosion. Rodeo concerts also have fireworks that scare barrel horses.

Grand Entries: Have lots of banners and flags that could spook your horse. Once your horse has been spooked, it is hard to get him to concentrate on his barrel run.

Crowds/Fans: The crowds and fans at rodeos are much louder than at barrel races, and the announcers encourage them to make all sorts of noise for the barrel racing. They seem to think it helps our horses, for some reason.

Arena Ground: The ground at rodeos is poor at best, and they rake only during slack. If there are twelve people in the performance, then they also rake only after every twelve runs in slack. They never rake during the performance with a tractor.

Other Event Contestants: Ropers and bulldoggers warm up at the same time as the barrel racers, and they are swinging their ropes around and jumping off their running horses. If your horse has never been around this, and even if he has, it can scare a horse and cause him worry.

Warm up Areas: In rodeo, it is very rare that you have a large enough warm-up area for all of the contestants, and most of the time, there is no warm-up area at all. When there is a warm-up area, the ground has usually not been worked up. You just have to find an area somewhere and try and warm up your horse the best that you can.

c. Keeping your horse sound

- Always do stretches before competition. This helps keep your horse from pulling a muscle.
- Always make time for proper warm-ups. This will insure that your horses' lungs are expanded enough to compete at his peak.
- Always condition your horse before you compete on him. If your horse is not in competition condition he cannot perform at his best.
- Always cool your horse down after competition. Your horse needs to continue moving for at least ten to fifteen minutes after competition to insure that his muscles don't lock-up.
- Always wrap your horse's legs if hauling two hours or longer. This helps support the tendons, and helps prevent muscle fatigue.
- Always use protective leg wraps on both the front and hind legs, even in the practice pen. If a horse over reaches or hits any of his legs it can cause serious bruises and lameness, even at a slow pace.
- Always clean your horse's feet before you put him in the trailer. If he has a stone, or even packed in soil in his sole, it can cause sole pressure or make a bruise which can cause lameness.
- Always check stalls at fairgrounds for safety before you ever put your horse in them. A piece of twine, loose board, wire or nail can cause serious damage to your horse.
- Always lift your saddle pad up to the bottom of your pommel before tightening your cinch. This keeps the saddle pad from causing painful pressure on the horses' withers when you tighten up your cinch.
- Never adjust your saddle by putting your weight in one stirrup. This can put your horse's spine out.
- Never run your horse straight into the gate when you finish your run. This causes un-needed stress on your horses' hocks. Turn at the gate in the direction of the last barrel when you get to the end of the arena, unless there is a run in/out alley or no room to turn.
- Never let your horse drink out of a fairgrounds stock tank. And make sure to clean out any water tank provided with Clorox. Stagnant water or water that has been sitting in a tank is a breeding ground for bacteria and your horse could get sick from the water.
- Have your horse re-shod regularly, every five to six weeks. Performance horses need to be re-shod more frequently than pleasure horses. A horses' toe grows out faster than his heels and can cause strain on his tendons and ligaments during competition if they are allowed to get to long.
- During wet weather or if your horse has to stand in a stall that might get moist, brush 7 percent iodine in the frog creases to prevent thrush or other bacteria. Even the mildest case of thrush can affect your horses' performance.

d. Pre-exercise stretches

1) **Forearm Stretches:**

Pick your horse's front knee up to be horizontal with his chest while letting the foot and ankle hang down from the knee, hold for a ten count. Make sure to keep the leg in front of the horse, never pulling it out away from the horses' side. Then grab his foot and extend his toe toward the ground, straightening his leg out, and hold his foot three inches above the ground for a ten count. Set his foot down gently; do not drop. Repeat on opposite front leg.

2) **Hamstring Stretches:**

Pick up a hind foot as if you are going to clean it out. Hold your horse's ankle and back up slowly, keeping his toe only two to three inches from the ground, bring his hind toe toward the back of his front foot. Once your horses' leg is stretched as far forward as it can go, set it on the ground and make your horse leave it there for a twenty count. Repeat on opposite hind leg. You will have to do this slowly so he can relax into it.

3) **Stifle Stretches:**

Pick up a hind foot while keeping the horse's toe just two to three inches off the ground. Take your knee/thigh and put it against your horse's hock. Extend his leg backward in the direction of his tail, all the while keeping the toe two to three inches from the ground. He will probably extend it the rest of the way on his own and stretch it himself. If not, be sure not to let him set his weight on his foot until it is brought back underneath him. Repeat on opposite hind leg.

4) **Top Line Stretches:**

Take a cookie or handful of grain and let your horse smell what you have. Get him to bring his nose back to his ribcage to get a bite. He should be flexing only his neck and spine; his feet should not move. Do this to both sides two or three times. Then bring your hand down between his knees and make him stretch his neck. Repeat several times.

5) **Free up your horse's hips and shoulders:**

Get your horse to walk in a tight circle with you standing at his hip. Make sure he is crossing over with the front feet as well as the hind feet. Repeat in both directions, until he is crossing over with both the front and hind feet. This may seem like a simple waste of time, but as a trainer, I have learned that if your horse is not freed up in the front and hind end before you tighten his saddle up, he has a hard time freeing up with the cinch tightened and you may just get bucked off.

All of these exercises should be done before you tighten up your cinch and get on to ride.

These exercises also allow you to notice any soreness your horse might have and give you time to take care of any problems before they become an issue.

e.   Pre-competition warm-ups

Your horse should already be in competition condition before you enter up to run, so don't use your warm-up time to condition your horse. Take the time to stretch and loosen up your horse's muscles before you start your warm-up. Your warm-up should take between twenty-five and thirty minutes. Your horse just needs to loosen up his muscles and get his adrenalin up to be ready for competition; he also needs to catch his breath prior to entering the arena.

Don't over warm-up your horse and wash him out.

1)   Stretches: four to five minutes.
2)   Free up hips and shoulders before you tighten up your cinch to get on.
3)   Long trots: ten to fifteen minutes.
4)   Walk and let your horse catch his breath, four to five minutes.
5)   Loping: ten to fifteen minutes.
6)   Sprints: three to five minutes, only when there is a safe place with good ground.
7)   Walking/Cool down/catch breath: ten to fifteen minutes prior to your run.

The warm-up time at a barrel race is not for training on your horse. If you think you need to train on your horse prior to a competition, your horse is not ready to be entered up yet. Forcing your horse to run the pattern five or ten times in the warm-up pen, only tires him out, and he will not have anything left when you finally do make your competition run. Go ahead and trot or lope around the barrels once or twice before your run, but don't run the legs off your horse on the pattern before you ever get in the competition arena.

f.   Conditioning for competition

For your horse to compete at the top levels today and stay sound, he has to be in excellent physical condition. If you were asked to go run in a marathon, you would not just show up the day of the competition and run. If you did, you would not perform very well, and you would be extremely sore for days to follow.

We have to look at our horses in the same light. Yes, they are naturally very strong and powerful athletes, but in order to perform split-second maneuvers and stay sound, they need to be in top condition to perform at their absolute best.

I start my conditioning training thirty days prior to any competitions that I plan to attend, as it takes approximately thirty days to get a horse in competition shape. Your horse will still need continuous workouts after that at least three times a week to retain his condition.

Week 1: Start out with forty-five minutes to one hour of light to medium riding per day for five days. This is all done out of the arena and consists of lots of long trotting. Start out with five to ten minutes of long trots, then five minutes of walking, and keep repeating for five days. Then give your horse two days off.

Week 2: The second week, I continue with lots of long trotting, but add hills and five to ten minutes of continuous galloping to start building up the lungs as well. Still work your horse five days on and two days off.

Week 3: By now, your horse should have built up some stamina. Push him harder in your workouts, and keep him in a long trot until he has worked up a good sweat and is breathing hard. Then let him walk for five minutes. Make him gallop until he is breathing hard and wants to stop, then give him five to ten minutes to walk it off. Long trot again as above, give him a walking break, then gallop as above, and rest at a walk. He should be able to continue this for an entire hour. Be sure to cool him down at a walk for the last fifteen minutes when you are done so he won't stiffen up and get sore on you.

Week 4: Start out the same as in week three, but after thirty minutes, take him to the arena and lope some circles, work on drills or exercises, or even make a barrel run or two for your final thirty minutes of the day. (Work your horse only five of the seven days of the week.)

Follow-up conditioning: To keep your horse in his competition condition, you only need to work him for one hour three days a week. The workouts should consist of one hour of the above week three or week four workout schedules. If you have a barrel race on the weekend, you can do only two workouts a week.

g.   Barrel racing bits

There are so many bit options for barrel horses that it can be mind boggling. The most important thing to remember is that most of your control is in your legs and balance, not in your horse's mouth. Barrel horses work differently than most horses because we use only one rein throughout most of our run. Therefore, we need to use a bit that works with one rein and doesn't send signals to the wrong side of our horse. The wrong kind of bit can be very detrimental. It's not just about stopping your horse; it's also about the ability to steer your horse.

Barrel racing bits need to have independent shanks, allowing you to send signals to your horse with one rein on one side at a time. They also need to have a gag that allows your horse to receive the signal and have time to react before the mouthpiece gets him. Barrel racing bits also need to have some lift so you can move your horse's shoulders and bend him at the ribcage without stopping him. Also, I prefer a dog-bone mouthpiece since a dog-bone mouthpiece works on the horse's bars independently and leaves room for the horse's tongue without pinching it. The dog-bone mouthpiece also helps keep the horse collected and tucked at the poll.

Every horse is different, and what works well on one horse may not work well on another. Therefore, I suggest you don't buy a bit just because it works well for someone you know on their horse. It is very important that you try that bit on your horse to see if it works well for him. It takes at least three times working your horse with a bit to actually know if it is working correctly, as your horse needs time to get the feel of the bit and learn how to respond to it. Therefore, I suggest trying the bit at least five times before you decide to buy it or get rid of it. Some bit makers will lend you a bit to try before you buy, and if not, most of your friends will lend you a bit to try for a week so you can find one that works for you and your horse.

Parts of the bit:

- **The shank:** Provides stop it bits. The longer the shank, the more leverage it has.
- **The purchase:** Provides lift in bits. The longer the purchase, the more lift it has.
- **The gag:** Provides a warning before the mouthpiece engages. The larger the gag, the more warning time before the mouthpiece engages.
- **The mouthpiece:** Provides communication to the horse from the reins. A smaller diameter requires less pressure and is more severe; a larger diameter requires more pressure and is not as severe.

h.   Shoeing barrel horses

I am not a certified horse farrier, and don't claim to know more than the professional farriers around the world. I learned early on in my career how to trim my horses so I could save money but left the shoeing to the professionals. I have always been there when my horses were being shod, watching and learning whatever I could. I felt that they were the professionals, so I let them shoe my horses however they felt best. I learned the hard way, at a very young age, how important it is to have your horse shod properly, when a very talented horse was permanently crippled by a bad shoeing job by a certified farrier.

With all of the new methods and products out there to choose from, making sure that your horse is shod properly is sometimes hard to determine. Over the years, I have tried some of the new fads, but it has always come down to how the foot is trimmed and not what was put on the foot that determined whether my horse stayed sound.

It has become more and more difficult to find a farrier who will listen to you and shoe your horse how you want your horse shod. They all seem to have their own way of doing things and don't like to be told how to do their job. And as far as I can tell, hot shoeing, cold shoeing, or whatever method they use to shape the shoe and put it on doesn't make all that much difference.

The most important thing I can tell you about your horse's feet is to make sure your farrier keeps your horse's foot level. The horse's heels have to be level with each other, and the angle of his hoof needs to be the same angle as his pastern for him to travel properly and stay sound. This is a fact.

If a horse's toe is left too long or cut too short, it causes severe strain on the tendons and navicular bone. If the bars are removed or trimmed too much, they can't act as a brace to control the expansion and contraction of the hoof to protect the frog. If the heels are contracted, they lose their ability to support the lateral expansion needed to handle the horse's weight and disperse the shock. And most of all, if the foot is not level and one side is higher than the other, it causes excess pressure all the way up the horse's leg and starts showing up in the muscles, all the way up to your horse's back.

For your reference, I have included some pictures of the horse's foot, correct angle, and hoof expansion of the horse's foot. If you can't get a farrier to work with you and your horse, you are much better off leaving him barefoot.

You can also have your horse trimmed for a barefoot natural shoe, where there is no actual metal shoe. The hoof wall is just left about one-quarter inch long all the way around. This works well if you don't have a lot of rocks where you ride.

Several years ago, I finally decided to start shoeing my own horses the way I wanted them to be shod, since it was getting harder and harder to find a farrier that would shoe them the way I wanted and when I wanted. It takes some time and patience to get good at it, but it is not rocket science, and there are a lot of good farrier schools out there that can teach you how to shoe your own horse in a relatively short time. And the cost of the school is saved in just one rodeo season if you have several horses, not to mention that it sure comes in handy when you lose a shoe at a rodeo and need it replaced right away.

It doesn't really matter what type of shoe you use; it just matters that the shoe is fitted properly to the horse's foot.

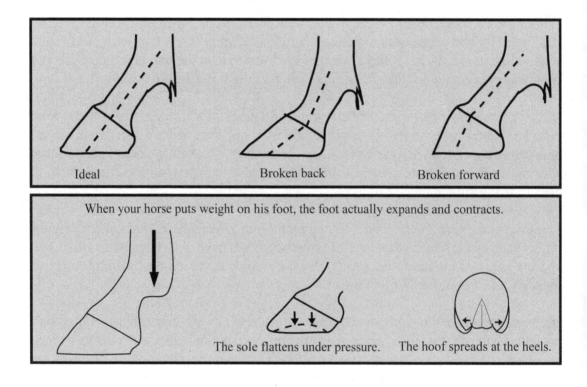

Ideal   Broken back   Broken forward

When your horse puts weight on his foot, the foot actually expands and contracts.

The sole flattens under pressure.   The hoof spreads at the heels.

i.   Helpful hauling tips
(things to keep with you at all times in your trailer)

Water purifier: You can find it at any RV store or Wal-Mart. Some horses won't drink water that has been heavily chlorinated or that has a strange taste, so if you put some purifier in the water, it takes away the chlorine taste and they will usually go right to drinking. If your horse does not drink enough water, it can cause colic and many other serious problems.

Pro-Bios: It is helpful to give your horse some Pro-Bios if he has to drink heavily chlorinated water, as the chlorine kills his natural antibodies and the Pro-Bios helps replace them.

Old set of shoes: Keep an old set of shoes that are not too worn out in your trailer. Your horse may throw a shoe at an event, and there is usually someone there who can put one on for you if you have it already shaped.

Small tools: Pliers and a hammer will help to fix stalls or pens to make them safe for your horse. A pair of fencing pliers works great because you can pull a nail out of a horseshoe or a fence and cut wire with them.

Tire pressure gauge: Proper air pressure saves fuel. Always check your tire pressure before you head out. Also make sure you have a good tire iron, the ones provided in most vehicles are worthless.

An old toothbrush and 7 percent iodine: If your horse has to be in a stall for several days, brush a little iodine in the creases of his frog. This treatment will keep him from getting thrush in his feet, or any other nasty fungus that may be growing in the stalls. Toilet tank deodorizer also works great for thrush, as it kills bacteria, but it hardens the sole and frog due to the formaldehyde in it. This is OK if your horse has soft soles, but too much use can make it hard to trim and pare out the sole and frog.

No-bow bandages and polo wraps: Wrap your horse's legs when you are hauling him, even short distances of one or two hours, and especially if he has to run once you get there. This gives his tendons support and slows down fatigue due to hauling. Try to get to your event early to let your horse's legs rest before you start your warm-up. Every hour your horse is in the trailer is the same as if he had walked for a mile.

Clorox: Use it for disinfecting water tanks. But be sure to rinse the tank well before you fill it up for your horse to drink out of.

Kotex pads or diapers: They make great sterile bandages for large wounds.

A medical first aid box for your horse trailer: Vet wrap, Betadine, gauze pads, thermometer, Banamine Paste for colic, etc.

PROFILE

Horses have been a lifelong passion for Jessi Mead. She was born and raised on a small ranch in Edgewood, New Mexico, where she grew up riding anything she could get her hands on. Jessi started competing in the local 4-H horse shows, gymkhanas, and junior rodeos when she was eight years old. At the age of twelve, she started working for a professional horse trainer at his Arabian horse breeding operation, where she learned everything she could about the horse breeding and training industry. She also read as many books on training horses as she could. But she attributes the success of her breeding program to the years she spent working with the professional trainer at his breeding facility. "During the years I worked for him, I learned more about training and breeding horses than I could have ever learned in a school or clinic."

She realized barrel racing was her calling, at the age of twelve, when her family brought home an old retired barrel horse. She learned how to ride this finished barrel horse and how to be competitive. So when her sister, Patti, gave her a two-year-old green broke quarter horse filly, she wanted to train it herself for barrel racing. She did just that and turned that filly into a very competitive mare in several events. Then at the age of fifteen, she bred her first mare and raised her first quarter horse. This was the start of her lifelong career in the equine industry.

Her decision to train her own horses for barrel racing had her looking for well-bred horses with the athletic ability to compete in timed events. Initially, she tried buying green-broke horses off the racetrack to finish training on the barrels. But she soon found out that getting the "racetrack" mentality out of these colts took a lot of time, and it wasn't usually very successful, as they often ended up lame from something that had happened in their race training. She did, however, learn from the experience which race horse blood lines were the most naturally disposed for barrel horses and decided to start breeding and raising her own barrel prospects.

The success she was having on the horses that she had raised herself brought her to the decision to start her own breeding program, where she could raise and sell good sound barrel horses that had the great racehorse breeding for speed but were crossed on foundation cow bred quarter horses for the needed agility in barrel racing. For many years now, she has been able to produce competitive and sound barrel horses for the barrel racing industry. She has won numerous titles, awards, and championships, and all on horses that she raised in her own breeding program. In the last thirty years, she has successfully trained over two hundred horses on the barrels.

Jessi still competes regularly and with the top barrel racers in the world at professional rodeos all over the western United States. While she prefers competing at professional rodeos since the purses are larger, she also competes in open barrel races, local jackpots, barrel futurities, and amateur rodeos. The difference between Jessi and other professional barrel racers is that she chooses to sell the horses that she has trained and competed on once she has them competitive at the top levels. This allows her to stay fairly close to home to be with her family and run her quarter horse breeding program.

Her extensive equine experience spans much further than just training barrel horses and competing on them. She also breaks all of her own horses and trims and shoes them all herself. For her breeding program, her duties range from breeding and foaling out mares to handling a breeding stallion and artificially inseminating mares. She has also competed in equine jumping competitions, shown at halter and pleasure, worked horses on a cart, shown Arabians in full dress competitions, driven draft horse teams, and competed in all of the timed events in women's rodeo. If it can be done on a horse or with a horse, no doubt, she has done it.

She is a lifetime learner, always willing to learn and try new ideas, and she isn't afraid to ask about what she doesn't know. When it comes to horses, she is like a sponge, filling her mind with knowledge that she might be able to apply somewhere in her existing program to keep her horses competitive and to continue to turn out champion after champion.

While Jessi has always taken pride in her ability to do all of the breaking and training on her own horses, she had major back surgery in 2001 and had to start letting someone else put the first thirty days on her colts. However, she still insists on doing all the rest of their training herself.

CPSIA information can be obtained
at www.ICGtesting.com
Printed in the USA
LVHW06s2315260318
571191LV00022B/368/P

9 781439 254615